RAND NATIONAL DEFENSE RESEARCH INSTITUTE

T0146301

Ramifications of DARPA's Programming Computation on Encrypted Data Program

Martin C. Libicki, Olesya Tkacheva, Chaoling Feng,
Brett Hemenway

Prepared for the Office of the Secretary of Defense/DARPA

For more information on this publication, visit www.rand.org/pubs/research_reports/RR567.html

Library of Congress Cataloging-in-Publication Data
ISBN: 978-0-8330-8514-6

Published by the RAND Corporation, Santa Monica, Calif.
© Copyright 2014 RAND Corporation
RAND® is a registered trademark.

Support RAND
Make a tax-deductible charitable contribution at
www.rand.org/giving/contribute

www.rand.org

Preface

Programming Computation on Encrypted Data (PROCEED) is a Defense Advanced Research Projects Agency (DARPA) program whose primary purpose is to improve the efficiency of algorithms that allow people to carry out computations on encrypted data—without having to decrypt the data itself. This allows people to entrust their data to others, and even get useful work done on the data, while providing a mathematics-based confidence that the data will remain private. RAND was asked to evaluate whether PROCEED—which expands the knowledge base of the global cryptographic community—is likely to provide more benefits for the United States than it does to its global rivals. Our assessment focused on the degree to which PROCEED technologies may be adopted, under what circumstances, and for what purpose. We then used the analytic framework generated to understand technological uptake decisions as a way of ascertaining how such factors would work in Russia and China vis-à-vis the United States (and, by extension, countries similar to the United States).

This research should be of interest to cryptography technology developers and funders, as well as analysts and policymakers focused on technology development and social impact, democratization, and Internet issues. This research was sponsored by DARPA and conducted within the Acquisition and Technology Policy Center of the RAND National Defense Research Institute, a federally funded research and development center sponsored by the Office of the Secretary of Defense, the Joint Staff, the Unified Combatant Commands, the

Navy, the Marine Corps, the defense agencies, and the defense Intelligence Community.

For more information on the RAND Acquisition and Policy Center, see http://www.rand.org/nsrd/ndri/centers/atp.html or contact the director (contact information is provided on the web page).

Contents

Figures and Tables

Figures

Tables

Summary

Programming Computation on Encrypted Data (PROCEED) is a Defense Advanced Research Projects Agency (DARPA) program whose primary purpose is to improve the efficiency of algorithms that allow people to carry out computations on encrypted data—without having to decrypt the data itself. This allows people to entrust their data to others, and even get useful work done on the data, while providing a mathematics-based confidence that the data will remain private.

Most of the PROCEED effort is focused on several technologies, including fully homomorphic encryption (FHE) and secure multiparty processing (SMP).[1] Both technologies impose performance penalties. The original instantiation of FHE took a hundred trillion (10^{14}) times longer to complete a calculation than it would have taken if the entire calculation were done without encryption. SMP also imposed comparable performance penalties, but they come in the form of multiple back and forth communications between the calculating node and the source of the data (10,000 to 100,000 loops is typical, although there are many potentially useful forms of SMP that use far fewer). DARPA's program aims to reduce these performance penalties substantially— for example, so that using FHE results in a 10^7 performance penalty instead of 10^{14}.

---

[1] Part of the PROCEED program also advances the computational art of "secret sharing," which is a way to do computations on data in which only part of that data is revealed at any one time. RAND did not examine that part of PROCEED.

Several plausible use cases have been identified for such technologies in ways that allow both parties to cooperate usefully while hiding their data from one another:

- cloud services
- satellite ephemera (knowing whether two satellites will collide or whether they have seen similar anomalies in the same place)
- map services (one party provides the map; the other, the origin-destination pairs)
- deconfliction of war plans by allies
- malware signatures (when the owner of the signatures wants to keep these signatures private)
- silent search warrants (that is, if material meets some sensitive criterion, a search warrant will be requested)
- watch list checks (so that passenger manifests private to the airlines and a sensitive target list can be compared)
- survey data consolidation.

The Decision to Use PROCEED Technologies

Our assessment suggests that the decision to adopt PROCEED technologies is unlikely to be an obvious decision. Rather, in light of its processing penalties, as well as the existence of alternatives, such a decision may be a close call in cases where it is adopted. For this reason, considerations that are normally of minor import in technology decisions may play a large role in differentiating adopters from nonadopters.

One reason such decisions are hard to make is that the level of trust in others that might justify using such technologies can be neither too high nor too low. If trust is high, then neither party has much cause to hide its data from the other. If trust is too low, then neither party has cause to trust the other with normal business arrangements associated with information processing (for example, will one side pay and the other deliver?) or even the data itself (how would one party know whether the data offered by the other party is correct, or is not shaped to make inferences about one's own data?).

Another reason such decisions are hard is that, faced with such penalties, people may conclude that they can bear the cost of information leakage (especially when leakage is so prevalent these days) by rationalizing to themselves that those who acquire such information may know more as a result but that they are very unlikely to then change what they do to the disadvantage of the data holder. They may also rationalize their choice by reflecting that some elements of their data are likely to leak in a secure transaction, even though the mathematics are valid. In other words, disclosure may not be a disaster, and security is never perfect.

A third reason is that people, when faced with the need to protect data on which calculations must be performed *and* the expense of using cryptography to do so, may search for novel alternatives: One might be using machines that start clean, are placed under mutual watch during use so that no inputs to their calculations can leak, and are then returned to a clean state when the project is complete. A second might be making extra efforts to find highly trustworthy parties to carry out such computations. A third might be to encrypt the metadata but reveal the data itself to the computational party, in the hopes that data without context is correspondingly far less useful to others.

Conversely, the viability of PROCEED technologies in the market will depend on how future cloud service providers price their services. A pricing structure that hopes to recapture costs based on how much storage is used rather than how much processing power is used is one in which the cost penalty for using PROCEED may be relatively modest.

Trust and Environments in Russia and China

Trust matters when economic actors cannot monitor each other's effort; lack of trust drives demands for data protection and encryption. Although both the cost of monitoring of how the trusted party protects sensitive information and the costs of using either FHE or SMP are high, businesses will decide to adopt PROCEED technology when they do not completely trust each other and when the cost of monitoring how data are handled exceed additional processing costs incurred through FHE or SMP. Because native trust varies from one culture to the next, so, too, will the relative costs of monitoring others vis-à-vis using PROCEED technologies.

As one way of understanding varied levels of trust, we examined the correlation between different types of trust and population demand for information about data encryption, information security, and data protection in Russia and China. These terms should be highly correlated with a population's interest in the PROCEED technologies. We collected an original data set that contains measures of cross-regional variation in trust and online search volume for "data encryption," "information security," and "data protection." In China, the demand for information about data encryption is higher in regions with lower levels of interpersonal trust (see Figure 3.3), whereas in Russia the demand for information about data protection and information security is higher in regions with lower levels of trust toward the government and law enforcement officials (see Figure 3.2).

This suggests that the diffusion of PROCEED technologies in China will by stimulated by the cultural factors, which remain persistent over time, and in Russia by popular attitudes toward authorities, which are less resilient. In both countries, the governments tightly regulate the encryption technology markets. Overall, we concluded that, given government approval of PROCEED technologies, their diffusion will be more rapid in China than in Russia.

Where Will PROCEED Be Taken Up?

In assessing the relative uptake of PROCEED technologies, we looked at both political and economic factors. Although adopting decisions are business cases, the differences between the United States, Russia, and China are both political and economic, with the former perhaps more enduring.

There are three political factors that strongly predispose PROCEED technologies to be taken up sooner and more broadly in the United States:

- Encryption is inseparably linked to the concepts of autonomy and confidentiality. The success of PROCEED technologies presupposes a population of data owners who want to choose a path somewhere between too little trust (wherein no data are exchanged, in part, because working relationships cannot be established) and too much trust (wherein no data are encrypted). The autonomy and ownership necessary to make these nuanced choices are more likely to exist in Western milieux than they are in authoritarian states.
- PROCEED technologies permit military coalitions to exchange data for coordination and deconfliction purposes without any party having to reveal its own plans. The United States has multiple alliances and access to many other coalitions. For Russia and China, allies and coalitions are far less important.
- PROCEED technologies may allow government agencies to process information for the purposes of surveillance without looking at it. Both the privacy of American citizens and the confidentiality of surveillance instruments can be preserved. If the processing indicates that a record is of interest, the United States may be able to make a probable-cause argument for releasing the full record in accordance with the Constitution, although there is disagreement about what information can be considered safe from government eyes absent such an argument.

In contrast with political factors that strongly predispose the greater and more valuable use of PROCEED in the United States, the four economic factors below, at most, weakly predispose the faster uptake of PROCEED in the United States in comparison to Russia and China:

- The demand for PROCEED technologies in Russia will be influenced by political conditions that affect overall trust toward the government, whereas in China, cultural norms will shape the diffusion of PROCEED technologies. Markets for encryption are more mature in China than in Russia. Encryption in general, and FHE in particular, is still the subject of discussion by only a handful of Internet users in Russia, whereas in China, the demand for the information about encryption is as high as the one for data protection. Correspondingly, adoption of PROCEED technologies is likely to begin earlier in China than in Russia, but neither would necessarily precede U.S. adoption.

- Although U.S. (more broadly, Western) firms tend to dominate the de facto standards-setting process, and standards facilitate the adoption of PROCEED technologies, standards tend to be lagging indicators (as they are more useful for consolidating a market than initiating one) and thus would play only a secondary role.
- If trends in favor of keeping national data from the hands of foreigners strengthen and deepen (as they may, given recently expressed foreign concerns over the reach of section 215 of the Patriot Act), countries could forbid certain types of data to cross their borders, thereby inhibiting the rise of services that amalgamate data or data services across borders. If so, PROCEED technologies may be used by service providers to convince sensitive countries that data leaving their countries in encrypted form are safe from disclosure. U.S. companies are far more likely to dominate such services than Russian or Chinese companies would.
- Over time, the diffusion of the PROCEED technologies in authoritarian regimes will depend on the patterns of their integration with the West. The uptake of PROCEED technologies will be faster in those authoritarian states whose organizations (e.g., corporations) are networked to Western organizations—but will be slower in the ones in which economic actors sit apart from Western organizations.

Conclusion

We cannot determine whether or not PROCEED technologies will be adopted in the face of the processing penalties that will be associated with using them—even if DARPA's program meets its technical goals. Our assessment indicates that although the prospect of being able to combine data from multiple parties or use third-party services while keeping data protected is an attractive one, there are many alternatives to using PROCEED that allow potential customers to make a range of trade-offs between economics and security. Nevertheless, there are many use cases for which PROCEED may be favored.

We judge that if PROCEED is adopted, it is likely to be adopted more rapidly in the United States (and similar developed countries) than it is in Russia and China, in large part because PROCEED is compatible with the U.S. political culture, and in smaller part because it better accords to the U.S. business environment.

Acknowledgments

We wish to thank the many people who have helped us put this product together.

First we would like to thank our DARPA sponsor, Drew Dean, who introduced us to this field of query and patiently explained the many ins and outs of processing encrypted data. Similarly, we would like to thank Ryan Henry, the co-principal investigator for the project, who helped shepherd this work from inception to conclusion. William Welser made many insightful observations in the course of co-coordinating both sides of the overall DARPA project. Finally, we have benefited greatly from the insights of our reviewers, Lily Ablon (RAND Corporation) and Joan Feigenbaum (Yale University), who saw matters in ways that contributed considerable detail to the manuscript.

Abbreviations

AES	advanced encryption standard
ATM	automatic teller machine
BGW	Boneh-Gentry-Waters
DARPA	Defense Advanced Research Projects Agency
EU	European Union
FHE	fully homomorphic encryption
FOM	Foundation for Monitoring of Public Opinion (*Fond Obshchestvennogo Monitoringa*)
GDP	gross domestic product
GMW	Goldreich-Micali-Wigderson
IaaS	infrastructure-as-a-service
IARPA	Intelligence Advanced Research Projects Activity
IBM	International Business Machines Corporation
IEEE	Institute of Electrical and Electronics Engineers
IT	information technology
MBA	master of business administration
NIST	National Institute of Standards and Technology

PaaS	platform-as-a-service
PRC	People's Republic of China
PROCEED	PROgramming Computation on EncryptEd Data
R&D	research and development
RSA	(originally) Rivest-Shamir-Adleman
SaaS	software-as-a-service
SMP	secure multiparty processing
TSA	Transportation Security Administration
USB	universal serial bus

CHAPTER ONE

Introduction

The purpose of encryption is to convert information into something that looks like gibberish to everyone else. This gibberish can be transported and stored, but it cannot be understood and, therefore, one would imagine, it cannot be processed. Amazingly, however, under some circumstances, encrypted data can in fact be processed, even if those doing the processing have no idea what the data say or what they mean. The Defense Advanced Research Projects Agency (DARPA) is currently running a technology development program, entitled Programming Computation on Encrypted Data (PROCEED), to enhance the state of the art in such processing.

PROCEED has three components. We focus on two of them: fully homomorphic encryption (FHE) and secure multiparty processing (SMP).[1] FHE permits one party to lend its data out, in encrypted form, to a second party who can then process the data (with or without data of its own) and return the answer, again in encrypted form. SMP allows two parties to manipulate or process each other's data vis-à-vis their own data without either having to share any unencrypted data.

---

[1] A third component of the PROCEED program is secret sharing, which allows multiple parties to collectively share a secret without any one party (or any group of parties below a certain size) knowing what the secret is. Secret sharing does not assume that data are encrypted, just sensitive. This report did not assess the relative impacts of secret sharing. As for SMP, some but not all variants use encryption; in some SMP protocols, including the celebrated Boneh-Gentry-Waters (BGW) protocol referred to in the first footnote in Chapter Two, sensitive data items are split into "secret shares" and the computation is performed in rounds on the shares, ultimately producing shares of the result, from which the entire result can be reconstructed by the appropriate party.

Although they emphasize different aspects of computation, FHE and SMP can be used on an overlapping set of problems.[2]

The basic question posed in this report is whether the PROCEED program, on a net basis, serves the interests of the United States. The reason that the answer is not obvious is that DARPA, via the program, is essentially supporting the development of mathematics (albeit of a particular kind). Even if the algorithms that employ the mathematics are generally proprietary, mathematics itself is a universal endeavor, access to which can be globally unconstrained unless explicitly classified (which there are no signs of in *this* program). Although mathematics has always circulated globally, the Internet now means that mathematical knowledge can diffuse instantly nearly everywhere.

Such a perspective raises the question of whether the PROCEED development program would create a particular advantage for the United States (notwithstanding that and how it might help everyone at the same time). The possibility that it has different advantages for different places arises because different countries and cultures may have different wants and needs for computation on encrypted data. RAND found such differences when analyzing DARPA's SAFER program (which was designed to allow warfighters and others a secure and reliable way to communicate over a system owned and operated by potentially hostile parties): Although everyone had access to the same technology, the technology was something that would help activists circumvent state censorship—but the only states that took censorship seriously were autocracies, not democracies. Hence, advantage democracies.

There is little *prima facie* basis for believing that the distinctions between the United States and other states (notably autocracies) are that obvious in the case of computation on encrypted data. Strictly speaking, a hard estimate would require forecasting how well *any* of PROCEED's technologies would be used. Unfortunately, while reli-

---

[2] One of the problems that might seem appropriate for FHE and SMP is that of searching for content among encrypted strings (for example, text). However, there are other algorithms that do as much with a far lower processing penalty. For this reason, we explicitly exclude string search applications among the use cases discussed below.

able numbers tell us how many people use circumvention technologies (for example, Tor[3]), there are no such numbers for FHE (which, to be fair, is a very recent invention) or SMP. Indeed, one of the only notable applications for SMP, despite its having been invented in the early 1980s, was permitting auctions for Danish sugar beet farmers.[4] Appropriately, DARPA seeks to improve the performance of these technologies to the point at which its use becomes cost-effective for a wider variety of purposes. But whether the improvements in performance will be large enough to affect usage by a given degree is a very difficult question to answer (and even harder to validate before the fact).

Instead, we intend to use this research report to tease out some of the underlying motivations that potential users might have, as well as explore whether differences in contexts (e.g., legal regimes) and cultures might predispose potential users in various parts of the world to adopt PROCEED technologies at different rates. To clarify the factors associated with using PROCEED technologies, we provide a representative sampling of potential uses in the following section.

Use Cases

The following use cases are provided, not as a canonical list, but by way of illustration so that readers can test their intuition against representative cases.

- *Cloud services:* Clients could encrypt the data they store with a cloud service provider but use PROCEED technologies to take advantage of the cloud provider's processing capabilities (especially if there are economies of scale in processing). Thus, they avoid having to download data back to their own machines for processing. They could also take advantage of the cloud's pro-

---

[3] See, for instance, Hal Roberts, Ethan Zuckerman, Jillian York, Robert Faris, and John Palfrey, *2010 Circumvention Tool Usage Report*, Berkman Center, October 2010.

[4] Ivan Damgård and Tomas Toft, "Trading Sugar Beet Quotas—Secure Multiparty Computation in Practice," *Ercim News 73: Maths in Everyday Life*, April 2008.

cessing capabilities whenever they are (1) unique, (2) sufficiently superior to what the client has, or (3) require data that the cloud provider has and will not release to the client.

- *Satellite ephemera*: Another use case, which is explored in greater detail in related RAND work,[5] is similar to the classic millionaire's dilemma.[6] In this case, two or more owners of satellites want to compare their projected orbits to determine the risk that one of the satellites will come too close to the other.[7]

- *Map services*: A client wants to be able to get from point A to point B without revealing these points to the map server. The map server wants to answer the client's question but without revealing the entire corpus of its own information—a body of knowledge that gives the map server a competitive edge in the marketplace. The client delivers the encrypted origin/destination pair to the map server, which then delivers an encrypted set of waypoints for optimal routing to the client.

- *Allies:* Countries that fight together may not necessarily want to share all of their information—but failure to do so may mean wasted effort, battlefield and/or surveillance gaps, and even increased risks of friendly fire. This use of PROCEED technologies would have each ally, in pairs or larger combinations, com-

---

[5] Brett Hemenway, William Welser IV, and Dave Baiocchi, *Achieving Higher-Fidelity Conjunction Analyses Using Cryptography to Improve Information Sharing*, Santa Monica, Calif.: RAND Corporation, RR-344-AF, 2014; David A. Galvan, Brett Hemenway, William Welser IV, and Dave Baiocchi, *Satellite Anomalies: Benefits of a Centralized Anomaly Database and Methods for Securely Sharing Information Among Satellite Operators*, Santa Monica, Calif.: RAND Corporation, RR-560-DARPA, 2014.

[6] A classic version of the secure multiparty processing problem arises from two millionaires who wish to determine whose wealth is larger but would prefer not revealing how much they actually had. If the dishonest millionaire knows that his counterpart is worth between $6 million and $10 million, he can narrow the range by offering that he has $8 million. The honest millionaire will be misinformed about the wealth of the dishonest one, and the dishonest millionaire will narrow down his estimate of the honest millionaire's wealth.

[7] That report also moots another use case in which satellite owners report the characteristics of anomalies registered by satellites, coupled with data on where these anomalies took place, to determine whether the source of these anomalies was internal to the satellites or external (and hence a function and thus indicator of, say, space climate).

bine the more sensitive portions of their war plans to determine the risks created when multiple parties act (or do not act) together. This use assumes the existence of algorithms that can usefully combine such data for the purposes of deconfliction, synchronization, sensor coverage, or the coordination of combined arms, for example. Note that in contrast to the satellite use case, each side is contributing a plan, rather than factual information, creating the possibility that one side can game another to get clues about what the other is really planning.

- *Malware signatures*: A customer receives incoming Internet traffic, some of which could be malware. It asks a government entity to review its traffic. The entity does not want to reveal the content of its Internet traffic to the government. The government, however, does not want to release its malware signatures to the entity because some of them are classified. In this example, we presume that the comparison of malware signatures to malware requires operations beyond those of a simple string search (the efficiency of which precedes the PROCEED program).

- *Silent search warrants*: The government wants to know whether potential bad guys possess particular evidence. The courts want to see probable cause before letting the government have unimpeded access to data protected through the Fourth Amendment. The government contributes an encrypted version of what it is looking for to a process that compares it to suspect data; the data are then combined to determine whether there is enough evidence for a search warrant.

- *Watch list checks*: When the watch list for airline travel was initially implemented, it was up to the airlines to match the names of people in their airline reservation system with the names of people on the watch list they were given. The Transportation Security Administration (TSA) was uncomfortable with giving airlines the names of these individuals, because it worried that some airline employees would leak the list to terrorists. In response, TSA developed Secure Flight, which had the airlines transfer information about their passenger lists to TSA so that TSA could do the checking. On behalf of the flying public, civil libertarians then objected to the government having access to individuals' travel details. PROCEED technologies could assuage both TSA's and the flying public's concerns by allowing lists to be compared without revealing each party's lists to the other.[8]

- *The Computer Research Association's Taulbee Survey*: A presenter at a January 2013 meeting of cryptologists presented a use case for PROCEED that entailed generating averages of salaries from computer schools without needing to know the individual inputs that went into these averages. In an America that is now more suspicious about what the government does with Census results, such methods may allow individual data to be hidden while statistics about such data are generated.

Use cases are not the same as uses; the latter requires entities to conclude that the benefits of meeting the various needs expressed above exceed the cost of doing so. We use these canonical use cases to illustrate, for the argument below, how the determinants of trust form the underlying determinants of technologies for processing encrypted data and how trust issues may differentiate users in various countries.

Organization of the Report

The remainder of the report tackles the related issues of the factors that go into choosing to use PROCEED technologies (Chapter Two) and how the core parameters of such a choice, notably trust, might vary between the United States and other countries, such as Russia and China (Chapter Three).

Chapter Two, on choice factors, asks: How does PROCEED, as a method of protecting the confidentiality of knowledge, compete with its alternatives? This chapter examines under what circumstances PROCEED is or is not more *objectively* cost-effective than alternatives. But,

---

[8] Although, as noted, there are more efficient technologies for string search than FHE or SMP, there may be person-matching algorithms that use more data than name-matching to account for the difficulty of matching names or the possibility of spelling and other variances between the name on the watch list and the name used by a passenger.

in practice, economic rationality is not an absolutely reliable[9] predictor of behavior, particularly when the logic required to make such calculations is sophisticated, the calculations themselves are complex, and the information such calculations are based on is extremely difficult to acquire. To make things fuzzier, because PROCEED is a technology of the future, the (unknowable) facts of the future must be taken into account as well. Nevertheless, such considerations can form a baseline, at least conceptually. The results of this chapter will be to sketch out circumstances in which PROCEED has superior characteristics and those circumstances in which it does not, as a way of suggesting that the adoption of PROCEED technologies contains much nuance and subtlety.

Chapter Three, on trust, will examine the different ways that trust enters in the decision to use FME or SMP, the different contexts for trust in each of the three organizational cultures and contexts (for example, legal regimes), and the extent to which, in these contexts, PROCEED technologies are likely to be perceived as continuous or discontinuous. This chapter is composed of several parts. First, we examine the literature on trust that deals with relationships between trust as socially influenced and the ability to carry out business in contexts that laws do not cover or circumstances in which people do not trust that the laws will, in practice, protect their interests. Where relevant, additional literature is summoned to explore how the fault line between continuous and discontinuous change—as perceived by potential users—shifts from one region to another. The chapter then examines the different trust and legal environments in two other countries: China and Russia. China's market has several salient features: a high reliance on U.S. service providers (to date), a low-trust business culture that favors business formation along familial lines but continues to evolve, the growing influence of commercial law (albeit from a low base), and a legal system that privileges government access to information and enforced cooperation by business firms (at least native ones). Russia's market has its own salient features: a somewhat high reliance

---

[9] This introduces the whole subject of behavioral economics, an accessible guide to which is Daniel Kahneman's *Thinking Fast and Slow*, 2012.

on U.S. service providers (except in the national security domain), an underdeveloped financial commercial sector, weak rule of law (which shows no signs of strengthening), a sophisticated cybercrime industry, and a strong security apparatus with strong de facto privileges to information and similarly de facto state participation in key sectors.

Chapter Four used the results of Chapters Two and Three to draw some tentative conclusions on whether the United States is likely to benefit from PROCEED to a greater extent—or at least before countries such as Russia and China might do so.

CHAPTER TWO

The Decision to Use PROCEED Technologies

What factors are likely to predispose organizations to adopt PRO-CEED technologies to protect their data, in light of the large processing penalty that computing on encrypted data entails? In addressing this question, we review the following issues:

- the complex logic of trust associated with processing encrypted data
- the value of confidential data
- possible leakages of encrypted data from processing it
- alternative methods of hiding information.

By way of caveat, although this chapter talks about PROCEED technologies as if FHE and SMP could be discussed interchangeably, FHE and SMP differ in where they take their processing penalties relative to computation on unencrypted data (or plaintext). With FHE, the processing stays entirely within the party that cannot read the encrypted data, avoiding communications costs but lengthening computation from anywhere between 10^{14} times longer (the state of the art before the PROCEED program started) to 10^7 times longer (DARPA's goal when the PROCEED program completes). With SMP, computation takes place as a back-and-forth process among the multiple parties.[1] However, the number of times each process goes back and forth is

---

[1] SMP protocols do not use keys per se. If two (or more) parties agree on the protocol (e.g., Goldreich-Micali-Wigderson [GMW], Yao, BGW, etc.), then running the protocol entails sending randomized messages back and forth. The messages one participant sends do

related to the size of the program as measured by the number of Boolean operations (also known as "gates") required to complete it. If communications latency is sufficiently low, then SMP can be a more attractive option. Conversely, if communications latency is high, then FHE may be more attractive. Another factor in choosing between the two depends on how much progress DARPA makes on FHE vis-à-vis SMP. The two protocols also differ in how they share the processing burden. SMP requires the participants to share in the computational burden, while FHE allows the client simply to encrypt its inputs (e.g., starting and ending points in a map problem), and the server then computes the outputs (e.g., an entire routing algorithm) from the encrypted input values. All variants of PROCEED technology impose heavy performance penalties, but the exact nature of the penalty varies with the technology. For example, the GMW protocol, which deals with zero-knowledge probabilistic proofs,[2] requires messages to be passed back and forth sequentially between participants. On the other hand, when using Yao's garbled circuit,[3] the messages can be grouped together into

---

not reveal any information to the other participant, but because they will never be explicitly decrypted, it is not really useful to think of them as encryptions. They exist merely as ephemeral bits of a larger secure computation.

[2] O. Goldreich, S. Micali, and A. Wigderson, "How to Play Any Mental Game," *Symposium on the Theory of Computing (STOC) '87*, 1987, pp. 218–229. Here is an easy example of a zero-knowledge proof: You want another country to prove that it has only ten missiles sitting in what you know are one hundred silos. The country does not want to reveal which silos are full (because such knowledge makes it easier for you to target these missiles). You both agree that you can choose one missile silo to examine at a time; between each look, the other country can shift its missiles from one silo to another. If enough examinations are carried out, you can assure yourself to within any level of statistical confidence that the country has only ten missiles; the country can assure itself that you do not know how its missiles are distributed among its 99 other missile silos.

[3] Andrew Yao, "Protocols for Secure Computations," SFCS '82, Proceedings of the 23rd Annual Symposium on Foundations of Computer Science, Chicago, Ill., November 3–5, 1982, pp. 160–164. Andrew Yao, "How to Generate and Exchange Secrets," SFCS '86, Proceedings of the 27th Annual Symposium on Foundations of Computer Science, Toronto, Ontario, Canada, October 27–29, 1986, pp. 162–167. Circuit garbling is a general technique for secure two-party computation, whereby one party prepares a "garbled" version of the function being computed. The two parties can then work together to evaluate the garbled function on their private inputs. The garbling process ensures that the output of the function

a small number of communication rounds. While both protocols have heavy computational and bandwidth requirements, the large number of rounds in the GMW protocol makes it more sensitive to network latency.[4] While each technology has different performance characteristics, the use of any PROCEED technology will entail a significant increase in running time when compared with the insecure calculation (e.g., an increase by a factor of 10^7).

The Complex Logic of Trust Associated with Processing Encrypted Data

The case for wanting to process encrypted data is one of mixed trust. Although each individual's input data can be protected from distribution and revelation, the output data that result from FHE computations on the input data cannot always be guaranteed to be correct. Take the map server use case. The client's source and destination can be protected from the map server's eyes, so to speak. Yet, the map server that is not trusted to see the input data is nevertheless trusted to calculate the optimal route from these input data. A similar type of trust is also necessary when using SMP. When calculating, for instance, a satellite conjunction analysis, the SMP protocol guarantees that each operator's orbital information is not leaked to the other operators— but it does not prevent operators from providing bogus inputs to the SMP protocol. To trust the outputs of the conjunction analysis calculation, one must trust the other participants to play fair. Computing on encrypted data removes the need for individuals to trust others with their secrets (e.g., one no longer needs to trust cloud servers not to read or disseminate personal data), but it does not remove the need for them

---

remains the same, but any intermediate values generated during the garbled computation will not leak any information about the parties' inputs.

[4] To maximize the bandwidth and minimize the latency between participants, it may be desirable to place each participant's hardware in the same physical location. Thus, each participant would have their own computer (possibly secured in a vault to which only they have access), but the physical proximity of these vaults would allow the computers to be connected using fast data lines (e.g., Ethernet cables).

to trust each other to provide accurate information (e.g., valid data in the case of SMP and valid algorithms in the case of FHE).[5]

Various techniques can be employed to mitigate this need for trust. An SMP protocol for conjunction analysis can be modified to reject any inputs incompatible with publicly observable orbital information. An FHE route-generation protocol that returns clearly suboptimal routes can also indicate cheating. In most cases, however, it is impossible to completely eliminate the need to trust that other participants provide truthful inputs to the protocol. PROCEED's tools can be viewed as a way to securely emulate a trusted third party—but with the same security drawbacks. For example, if a trusted third party cannot identify bogus data from one of the participants, then neither can the corresponding cryptographic protocol. If the output of the computation leaks information (e.g., a nontrivial probability of two satellites colliding shares concrete information about the whereabouts of such satellites), then using tools from PROCEED will leak the same information. On the other hand, whatever techniques the trusted party could use to mitigate this information leakage can also be implemented by using tools from PROCEED.

To understand the basis for paying the price for processing on encrypted data, therefore, one needs to divide the world not merely into trustworthy and not trustworthy parties, but into a third category that includes the partially trustworthy.[6] Consider how a holder of

---

[5] Confidentiality, integrity, and accessibility (CIA) is the accepted approach to information security. PROCEED technologies are almost entirely about confidentiality, but this section (alone) does examine some considerations associated with integrity.

[6] The trust relationships described above differ slightly from standard cryptographic notions of "fully malicious" and "honest but curious." Honest-but-curious parties will follow the protocol honestly—i.e., by sending the messages they are supposed to. Honest-but-curious parties may or may not provide "valid" inputs. When tests exist to determine whether inputs are valid (e.g., comparing satellite orbital information to the visible location of the satellite), these verifications can be incorporated into the secure computation. When no such verification strategies exist, cryptography cannot create them, and parties may introduce invalid inputs to the protocol to attempt to glean extra information. Malicious parties may refuse to send messages, or they may send messages that are formatted incorrectly or are carefully designed to trick the other participants into revealing information. Cryptographic tools exist to check whether participants are following the protocol (though they cannot check the

sensitive information may regard potential partners that are variously trustworthy, untrustworthy, and partially trustworthy:

- To those who are sufficiently trustworthy, one can reveal information without needing encryption (except to protect against intermediate third parties who have no need to see or manipulate the data—e.g., man-in-the-middle attacks).

- To those who are untrustworthy, one might hesitate for several reasons to reveal data even if these data are and stay encrypted. One is the risk of being cheated from a business perspective: A large percentage of trust transactions (at least in the United States) involve services rendered, either for money or for some less tangible reward. Another reason for hesitation is fecklessness—if those to whom one entrusts such data do not take the time and trouble to process or make such data available in a reliable and timely way. Or seriously untrustworthy people could return an answer that looks right but is actually wrong through incompetence or, worse, malice. This risk is reduced if there are ways of detecting a definitely wrong answer that can expose the other party; the other party, understanding as much, would be loath to cheat, but this is no guarantee against the processor failing to invest the resources to ensure that the data are correct. Conversely, if a third party is providing the data (for comparison, for instance) but not the processing (as with SMP), he or she may provide data that is incorrect but is shaped to determine what the other party's data are. All of these concerns introduce a complicated set of considerations associated with deterring wrongdoing, suggesting the wisdom of avoiding untrustworthy people if one can do so.

- Finally, there are the people who are trustworthy enough to be *provided* with correct data (for SMP) and/or correct processing (for FHE) but not trustworthy enough to *reveal* the data to. Furthermore, the case for SMP presumes that no third party that is

---

validity of their inputs). Thus, cryptographers can move from the honest-but-curious setting to the malicious setting (this just imposes an additional computation and communication overhead).

trusted by both parties exists (among those who have the requisite processing, storage, and communications capabilities), or at least that finding and working with such an individual is sufficiently difficult in comparison with bearing the computational penalties of using PROCEED technologies.

Only if one is in the last category can one begin to justify paying the costs for processing on encrypted data. Thus, the case for FHE and SMP depends on a very nuanced trust context. Consider, for instance, a situation (e.g., cloud services) in which one party, the client, has data, and the other party, the server, has storage, processing, and security capabilities. The client wants the data to be manipulated and trusts the server to do it correctly, but it does not trust the server not to peek at the data.

Though trust is required for social and/or legal reasons, it is complicated to define; it is not a mathematical construct. Furthermore, it is broader than just keeping the particular data secret. First, the very relationship itself will reveal some information. By entering into an FHE cloud arrangement, a client (or at least its cut-out [i.e., its mutually trusted intermediary]) tells the cloud provider of its existence, something of its economics and something of its security consciousness (because it is willing to pay a premium to keep its data secure *from the cloud provider itself* and it has no preferred alternatives), perhaps the size of its data, and even the frequency with which new data arrive.[7]

Furthermore, trusting the cloud service provider with the data and relying on it for computations while not trusting it not to look at the data is a highly nuanced notion of trust—because *any* business relationship requires some degree of trust if it is to function at all. There has to be trust in the probity of financial accounts and in the fundamental honesty of the cloud provider (e.g., not doubling fees or holding the calculations for ransom until the bills are paid). There also must be trust in the competence of the cloud providers—which

---

[7] These can be hidden to some extent by padding. If the client always sends some large block of encrypted data at regular and frequent intervals, the server will know only the upper bound on the amount of data and the frequency of updates.

would be reflected in the reliability of the computations (they can be checked, but that also adds costs) and in the continuous availability of the service.

Consider, by way of illustration, what would happen if external events reduced the trust that all parties had in one another. This could persuade data-holders in the cloud to shift from computing in the clear to using PROCEED technologies because they would no longer trust their cloud providers not to peek. But it could also persuade data-holders who were already using (or considering using) PROCEED technologies to shift toward taking the data in house, because they would no longer trust their cloud providers to do business honestly. The same indeterminacy would apply if external events (or simply a prolonged absence of negative external events) increased societal trust. Data-holders may abandon PROCEED technologies and compute without encryption—or data-holders may outsource their data but adopt PROCEED technologies because there are limits on how trusting they will be. In either case, if the economics of using PROCEED technologies are unfavorable, decreased trust may persuade data-holders to insource computations that were done in the clear, and vice versa—completely skipping over the intermediate option represented by PROCEED.

Although trust issues vying with processing penalties are the primary drivers of PROCEED technologies, other considerations may factor in. One consideration is that only by encrypting data can one entity share data with another. Thus, this technology allows computations to take place that would otherwise be forbidden. The difficulty is that, at present, laws that forbid data from being exchanged do not allow exceptions for encrypted data—which makes sense today because the recipient cannot use the encrypted data but might make less sense if and when PROCEED technologies come of age. The same caution may apply to longstanding policies to which such organizations adhere or to contracts that enjoin such information exchange. The benefits from transfer would have to overwhelm the caution that organizations may exhibit when an act looks as though it was unlawful or violated a contract.[8] An additional consideration, conversely, is that organizations may be reluctant to receive data that they have not scrubbed for reasonableness. In a sense, this is a matter of trust. The problem is solved if the receiving organization trusts a third party's competence at scrubbing data and the providing organization trusts the same third party's ability and willingness to keep the data confidential—but no such third party may exist that satisfies both criteria. The problem may also be solved if the data could be scrubbed algorithmically; if so, the data provider may apply the algorithm, or the algorithm may be applied by the recipient by converting the plain-data algorithm into one that works with encrypted data. However, if the recipient believes that data inputs can only be truly scrubbed by having a person check the data, then it will not find encrypted data adequately useful for its purposes.

The Value of Confidential Data

The next step in understanding the objective benefits of PROCEED and thus potential factors that would predispose its use is understanding the purpose of encryption. To wit, people use encryption to keep data from others—thereby raising the question of why doing so is worthwhile. There are several ways to answer the question: some easy, others hard.

An easy (or, at least, straightforward) case arises when data are entrusted to an entity with the expectation that the entity will protect the data from disclosure (this case represents the safeguarding entity's perspective, not the data owner's). Whether or not the data owner's desire to protect such data from disclosure is based on a thorough consideration of the costs and benefits is irrelevant, or, at most, secondary. The holder of such information only has to understand the legal ramifications (e.g., lawsuits, jail time), the business costs (e.g., no further data come in), or the social/psychological costs of violating a trust to under-

---

[8] See Joan Feigenbaum, Benny Pinkas, Raphael Ryger, and Felipe Saint-Jean, "Some Requirements for Adoption of Privacy-Preserving Data Mining," PORTIA Project White Paper, April 2005.

stand the risks entailed in providing less than 100-percent protection for such information.

The harder case is when one's own data are involved (or more commonly, the organization's own data). We encrypt because we do not trust others. Individuals value personal privacy for personal reasons, many of which have little to do with the potential for monetary loss. In some cases, we encrypt because we know that any person who seeks our information is very likely to be untrustworthy (e.g., hackers looking to steal credentials). Organizations must then ask what bad things can happen if others get their hands on the data. The answer seems like it should be that they *would* do things that they could not do before—but the better answer is more probabilistic: They *could* do things that they could not do before.

As an example of "would," consider a criminal who knows that you have a large sum of money in your account, access to which is predicated on your presenting a password. The criminal wants the money and would gladly take it, but lacks the password. Once armed with the password, the criminal can take the money and implement a decision that he or she has already made, but could not implement earlier. In this case, the decision to act has already been made, but the odds of success rest on the missing knowledge.

In many other cases, however, "could" is the better descriptor. Assume that you are in business, developing a product with sensitive parameters. Competitors who get their hands on such parameters would not only know what kind of products they may have to face in coming months, but also what technical challenges you think can be solved cost-effectively. Such knowledge, in turn, shapes which research and development (R&D) strategies they employ and which products they may offer to compete with your products. Knowledge of your plans may not necessarily mean that this competitor does something different—but it could. The term "could" suggests that the range of decisions available to the competitor is not only expanded as a result of having stolen the parameters, but that such knowledge alters the likelihood of their making a particular decision. It is entirely possible that, having absorbed such confidential information, they go ahead and do what they would have done anyway (indeed, for psychological reasons, people tend to use information for confirmation), but unless those with the confidential information know otherwise, they must assume that the consequences of changing the odds of a decision are tantamount to the consequences of changing a decision multiplied by the odds that the decision changes.

This perspective allows one to put a (highly notional) number on the value of protecting information.[9] It follows from the premise that (1) the failure to successfully employ a particular protection method (e.g., encryption) changes the likelihood that someone knows data that he or she did not know before, which, in turn, (2) changes the knowledge base upon which a decision is made, which (3) changes the decision, and (4) in ways that are unfavorable to you.

In some cases, the chain of consequence is direct and unbroken. Your failure to protect the integrity of your computer allows others to acquire your banking password (step 1), telling them something that they could previously only guess (step 2), allowing them to impersonate you *correctly* (step 3), which leads to the theft of your savings (step 4).[10]

In other cases, the chain of consequence is indirect and highly probabilistic, and the chain between the data acquired and the knowledge required has several internal steps—each whose probability is less than 1.0, and in some cases far less. Here, your failure to encrypt an email on your work computer leads to its interception within the local area network. This email, let us suppose, suggests that the decision to reinforce a Marine unit slated to a base in the Far East has yet to be made, suggesting that the decision to put a major command-and-

---

[9] For a more detailed version of the argument that follows, see Martin C. Libicki, Brian A. Jackson, David R. Frelinger, Beth E. Lachman, Cesse Cameron Ip, and Nidhi Kalra, *What Should Be Classified? A Framework with Application to the Global Force Management Data Initiative*, Santa Monica, Calif.: RAND Corporation, MG-989-JS, 2010, notably Chapter Two.

[10] The decision to impersonate you can be understood in two ways: Without the information, impersonation would have failed—so the change in the decision is the difference between impersonation with the right password or impersonation with a random, likely incorrect password. Or, without the information, impersonation would not have been attempted, so the information changes what was a decision not to try impersonation to a decision to try impersonation. For both cases, the broader point remains.

control center on that base is not as solid as reported. This may lead an adversary state to redeploy surface ships in a different fashion than it would have, which means that it could be in a better position to take advantage of a potential regional crisis that might occur if the United States were to deny rumors that it was prepared to reinforce the base. Note the long chain of inference and the relatively low likelihood that any one change in the likelihood of a step in the chain leads to a change in status at the next level. Yet, while the inciting event of this chain was small, the consequences of losing advantage in a crisis could be enormous: low probability multiplied by high consequences. There are probabilities at issue, which indicate that the decision to suppress information (that is, encrypt internal email) *is just one way of many ways to alter the odds of an adverse adversary decision* (e.g., one can create false information to mislead them, or change their incentives to do things one way rather than the other). Furthermore, there may be more than one chain of causality (perhaps the decision not to arm the marine brigade with a particular capability spoke to the usefulness of the capability as well, which then forces a change in their corollary-of-forces assessment), and these chains may be interlinked (one inference makes a decision more likely, but another inference from the same day may make a decision less likely).

Thus, although people may posit that the need to guard information is absolute and priceless, trade-offs must be made everywhere. When the cost of keeping information confidential is paid in terms of additional processing and/or communications time, then it may merit reconsideration.

Furthermore, as the next section suggests, even using PROCEED technologies does not completely assure that the data will not be revealed.

Possible Leakages of Encrypted Data from Processing

The potential for information leakage always exists, even when using cryptographic methods. The success of encryption is related to more than just key length (as will be explained further below). In addition, even if the encryption is sound, a not-completely-trustworthy partner can be a source of data leakage when using encrypted data in computation.

In theory, cryptography takes plaintext and gives it a level of security associated with the expected time required to crack the cryptographic key. Because the cracking time rises as the key length increases—often exponentially, or at least faster than any finite polynomial function (super-polynomially)—it is possible to achieve (or surpass) any desired cracking time (as a proxy for security) by choosing a sufficiently long key.

However, the length of the key is only one factor of many security determinants. Here is a partial list of others:

- the correctness of the cryptographic protocol
- the quality of the implementation of the cryptographic protocol
- the quality of key management
- the trustworthiness of the computer that stores and processes the data[11]
- the ability to handle plaintext without compromising emanations
- the probity of those handling the data.

Irrationally, potential users may also distrust the mathematics behind encryption even if such mathematics is provably sound.

So, while the claims that implementations of FHE and SMP funded by DARPA do not leak data can be verified using mathematical techniques, some data leakage is unavoidable in the process of computation. For instance, a service provider may be able to extract a few bits of information from an FHE calculation it has been asked to run by timing how long it takes to execute a process. Although there are defenses against such leakage, they are not without cost, such as raising the run time to a level characterized by the worst-case example.[12]

---

[11] One of the advantages of FHE is that it allows someone with a trustworthy system to forward encrypted data to a second party without fear that the computer carrying out the calculations on encrypted data has been compromised.

[12] For instance, a Quicksort with randomization takes time proportional to $n \log n$ on average versus n^2 as a worst case. By way of analogy, assume that you are trying to guess where

In all fairness, however, a few bits of insight into a seriously large database are unlikely to inform any adverse decisions—unless the cloud provider has narrowed down the potential contents of the database by other means (e.g., through human intelligence) and only wants to know whether it is this one or that one (that is, which human source is being listened to).

Bit extraction of a different sort is also possible with SMP. Consider the use case in which one party provides an origin and a destination, and the other party has a method for generating a safe route from your data. Neither wants to share its information with the other. However, the first party is curious about what criteria the second party uses to generate safe routes. So it feeds the second party a set of concocted origins and destinations in ways that, little by little, reveal details of the second party's routing judgments.[13] The ability to do this depends, of course, on context. Consider, by contrast, the problem of whether two satellites will run into each other. If you, as a satellite owner, wanted to determine where someone else's satellite is exactly, when you only know the location approximately, you could conceivably invent a satellite of your own and carry out a conjunction analysis that gives you the probability that a crash will occur—but unless your satellite is otherwise invisible, the other party will know that the data are faked if they do not match the other party's prior knowledge about your satellite that can be drawn from what can be observed in the sky (unless one party

---

something sits in a long narrow room. Your only evidence is that someone has gone into the room, copied a number that is on the item, and returned with the number. If one assumes that this person went about this task expeditiously, then one can guess its approximate location in this long narrow room by guessing how long it would have taken to walk in, copy the number, and walk out. This person can defeat such a method by lingering in the room long enough to get to the end of the room and back—but only at the cost of taking longer to carry out the task. By first converting each calculation to a circuit form, and then computing the circuit, most forms of FHE and SMP eliminate time-to-complete estimates as a form of leakage. Indeed, this is one reason why secure computations require significantly more time than insecure computations.

[13] Note, however, that the client's start and stop locations are not subject to this type of leakage, as the mapping server receives no output from the protocol. In that sense, the leakage is asymmetrical.

says it wants to run the SMP analysis to determine in what orbit to launch its satellite).

The point of these excursions is not that encrypted data is no longer encrypted if one can perform computations on them, but that the choice in security is not between catastrophic revelation and no revelation, but between more or less. Even perfect[14] security as judged by the standards of the cryptographic protocol is not perfect when implemented. Conversely, even complete openness is not necessarily disastrous (imposed legal obligations to protect data aside) if others are unlikely to change their decisions as a result of what they find out.

Note that this is a normative rather than a positive analysis. Just because logic suggests that security is a matter of degrees rather than absolutes does not mean that individuals and organizations will approach security as a matter of probabilities rather than absolutes. Thus, the considerations that go into the trade-offs discussed below may well be decided by those who believe that nothing short of unbreakable security will do—regardless of the low likelihood of adverse actions resulting from imperfect security. However, when it comes to *evaluating* the adoption of FHE and/or SMP, some consideration should be given to what users actually get out of it in terms of the cost to them of losing confidentiality.

Alternative Methods of Hiding Information

In examining the alternatives to PROCEED technologies (so as to avoid the processing penalties), we consider several use archetypes. First is a cloud service, in which one party contributes the data, and the other party (the cloud service provider) contributes storage and processing, but no data that it wants hidden.[15] Second is an asymmetric process

---

[14] That is, the average time required to extract the information is adequately long.

[15] In recent years there has been a growth of applications that are only offered as cloud services, and, in some cases, have features that are not found in shrink-wrapped or downloadable form (see an interesting discussion on Prezi, one such application, in Bruce Schneier's blog post, "Terms of Service as a Security Threat," of December 31, 2012). In some cases the terms of agreement allow these applications to use your data freely for their purposes, sug-

in which both parties contribute something fundamentally different: e.g., the mapping user case or the malware signatures. One of the contributors is the client (e.g., the person with the start/end coordinates) and the other is the server (e.g., the person with the router-creation program). Third is the symmetric process in which both parties contribute something analogous to the calculation (e.g., the satellite conjunction case, the allies case).

We start with the cloud computing case. What are the client's choices?

- Using FHE
- (Own) Using the client's own capabilities for storage and processing
- (Part) Using the cloud for storage but pulling the calculations in house (the economics of which depend on the cost of communications vis-à-vis the cost of computation and the comparability of the client's algorithms vis-à-vis the server's algorithms)
- (Trust) Trusting the service provider (while encrypting the data in transit and perhaps employing ways to determine that the service provider is not malicious).

Assume for the moment that the requirement for security is non-negotiable. What would have to be true about the economics of processing to shift the balance in favor of FHE vis-à-vis in-house processing? If, for instance, the performance penalty for using FHE is 10^7, then the relative advantage of outsourcing has to be comparably high to tilt the decision to FHE. Consider some possible situations:

One is that the server has algorithms that the client does not have.[16] Such algorithms, by their very nature, would not be in the public domain, or if they were in the public domain would be suf-

---

gesting that their value proposition comes from their accessing your data. Such applications, at this point, do not seem to lend themselves well to cryptographic techniques that permit the data to be manipulated without the cloud provider knowing what the data are—or at least there is no good incentive to do so.

[16] From a mathematical perspective, this is tantamount to saying that the server has a private input—whether the input is an algorithm or data is secondary.

ficiently hard to replicate on the client's machines. To wit, there are
no turnkey solutions (or at least none that the client could afford to
purchase). That may be true if the algorithms were sufficiently arcane
and specialized or, alternatively, if they were proprietary and the service provider declined to convert them into something marketable. A
variant on that possibility is that the algorithm requires a high degree
of real-time maintenance (as might be true for a mapping program)
or, what is similar, continual improvement (as might be the case for
language translation). This leaves FHE or Trust as the only practical
solution.

Another is that the cost of computation (and the implied cost of
waiting for an answer) is low compared to the costs saved from using
cloud services. There may be economies of scale in data hosting. Alternatively, using a cloud may mean less need to risk capital, hire a staff,
rent a building, establish web connections, and deal with security
issues.[17] The economic case for FHE is better if the alternative of sending the data back for processing is infeasible because the data volumes
are large. Clearly, though, the baseline computation costs[18] might be
such a minute fraction of the overall cost of the cloud services that a
hypothetical 10^7 increase in the costs of computation would still not
bring overall costs up very much.

To give a rough order-of-magnitude sense of when large increases
in the cost of processing may be readily absorbed, we posit a cloud provider who bills as much for computation on a machine as for storage
that fills the machine's hard drives. Now imagine a client who wishes
to grind the numbers of an annual report, needing a machine's worth
of data storage but only 100 milliseconds worth of the same machine's
computational capability once a year (assume further that a machine's

---

[17] This statement presumes that cloud service providers can specialize in providing server-
side security services in ways beyond the capabilities and budgets (not to mention management attention) of smaller enterprises.

[18] Waiting a billion times longer for a calculation to finish may sound like an enormous
penalty, but if the normal calculation would have taken 10 nanoseconds, and the FHE calculation would have taken 10 seconds, the additional wait may be completely acceptable
in some environments. The same seven-orders-of-magnitude difference between one second
and 30 years, however, may be deemed unacceptable.

worth of storage costs as much as a year's worth of processing). If the client wants to use FHE, with its 10^7 time processing penalty, then the 100 milliseconds becomes a million seconds, or roughly a week and a half (less, if it pays to use parallel processing). The cost, if proportional to processor usage, of computation is now 3 percent of the (unchanged) cost of storage. This may get the cost of FHE into the ballpark of consideration. That noted, the current pricing model for commercial computing clouds, such as Amazon EC2, is to charge by the hour (with higher charges associated with faster machines) rather than per storage. Thus, pricing models would have to evolve in the opposite direction if they are to get most of their revenue from data storage and little if any of their revenue from processing.

The attractiveness of FHE also depends on *other* arrangements that a cloud provider might make with particularly security-conscious clients as a way of gaining their business.[19] As an alternative to FHE, cloud providers could set aside some part of its cloud as a physical enclave in such a way that the client could detect any access of the data on the part of the cloud provider.[20] Or, going further, it could keep the data encrypted but allow clients to keep on premises a tamper-proof processor[21] that decrypted the data, carried out computations on it, encrypted the results, and returned them to the original database. To be sure, neither option is a complete and costless substitute. On the one hand, clouds get their economies of scale from being able to leverage

---

[19] Whether it would actually make the attempt to offer such a client a way to assuage its security fears without having to suffer such a large computational penalty may depend on how competitive the market is, and how sticky the current relationship is between the client and the cloud provider. The latter may prefer not to make special arrangements and profit from selling millions of times more computational processing to the client.

[20] This is tougher than it looks. The machine would have to be closely watched by both parties, especially when it is being maintained. The machine would have to be rigorously inspected to guard, for instance, against the provider surreptitiously inserting a cable or an antenna. It would also have to be locked and continuously monitored to ensure that parts are not sneaked in and out—particularly during its inevitable maintenance.

[21] The idea of building multiparty computation from tamper-proof hardware has been studied. See Goyal, Vipul, Yuval Ishai, Amit Sahai, Ramarathnam Venkatesan, and Akshay Wadia, "Founding Cryptography on Tamper-Proof Hardware Tokens," *Theory of Cryptography: Lecture Notes in Computer Science*, Vol. 5978, 2010, pp. 308–326.

common facilities and manpower, and some of that advantage is lost when customers get special arrangements (particularly if these arrangements have their own hardware requirements). On the other hand, while one can generate mathematical proofs of the security of FHE processes, everyday security often boils down to two factors that do not lend themselves well to proof one way or the other: How badly does the curious party want to get its hands on the data, and what tricks does it have up its sleeve that the other side would not anticipate? In other words, if clients did not trust the cloud provider, can they confidently trust the arrangements that the cloud provider might offer for its suspicious customers?

Consider next the asymmetric two-party case. Here the cloud server has information without which the client's calculations will not work: e.g., the mapping use case. In such circumstances, the client cannot use its own servers for the calculations, or, at least, not without some degradation in the quality of answers. This leaves the client's other choices as follows: to use FHE/SMP (depending on the nature of the calculation among other factors) or just to trust the server not to be overly curious.

This case, however, raises the issue of how well the server can protect *its own* secrets even if it uses PROCEED technologies. These cryptographic technologies can ensure that no information is revealed *beyond what is revealed by the output of the computation alone.* Since every answer represents leakage of some sort, even PROCEED technology may not provide sufficient privacy in certain situations. For instance, if the client wants to cross a river safely, and its route takes one bridge when it could have taken (or, based on geography, should have taken) a bridge that was more direct, the client may infer that the bridge not chosen was particularly dangerous. Such an inference may not necessarily be completely certain, though; perhaps the neighborhoods to the north or to the south of the bridge should have been avoided, and if a different set of origins and destinations were offered for analysis, that particular bridge may have been chosen (because such neighborhoods could be more easily skirted). If the client wants to know, with greater justification and confidence, what the server knows about the conditions at that bridge, it could submit a large number of origin and destination pairs. With each pair, the client would gain greater knowledge about what would otherwise be the server's proprietary data. There are, of course, limits to such a game. The server may conclude that the volume of requests indicates an overly curious client and limit its access. If the server charges a nontrivial fee for each run (not implausible if using PROCEED is computationally expensive), then the client's curiosity may be costly. Or the routes served could be suboptimized or randomized in subtle ways[22] that provide the client most of what it wants but throw off the inferences that the client might make about the server's data. Regardless of how the game goes, or whether it even commences, the point (again) is that not even perfect cryptography can afford perfect security.

Alternatively, the client can use analogous redundancy techniques to maintain an adequate level of ambiguity in the server owner's mind (about the true origin-destination pair) without having to use PRO-CEED technologies. The trick is having some guess about what the server's owner (or, perhaps more accurately, those to whom the server might provide data) plans to do with the data. Consider a stark example: The client is afraid of assassination by a drive-by shooting—and cannot be sure that the server has not been compromised by friends of the assassination team. But the drive-by shooters only have one team to send out against the client. If the team chooses a random street hoping the client would drive by, its odds of getting the client are very low—let us assume so low that it would abandon the attempt (perhaps the odds of being arrested on a weapons charge overwhelm the low odds of completing the mission). Thus, any information that would help it focus its efforts would be quite valuable—hence the value of tapping into the server's results, which generate, in the clear, the optimal route for the client to use at a particular time. The client, suspecting as much, however, wants to generate as many routes as possible—ideally, a set that collectively tells the drive-by shooting team that the client could be anywhere (or at least in so many possible places that no ambush is possible or at least worthwhile). If the cost of generating a million pairs using unencrypted data seems high, it may nevertheless be lower than the cost

---

[22] In this particular case, the facts on the ground could plausibly change from one model run to the next.

of generating a pair using encrypted data if the time required for processing is ten million times longer—but it is also necessary to account for the cost and difficulty of generating bogus origin-destination data in determining whether this is a worthwhile alternative.

This game has countermoves. The server may already have some prior knowledge about the client's origin-destination pairs. It may not know, for instance, what the exact origin and destination is, but it may figure that the latter exists in a particular neighborhood. This could allow it to rule out, say, 99 percent of the asked-for origin-destination pairs as phony, meaning that the client would have been no worse off with a smaller set (10,000 in this case) of pairs (as long as they all looked plausible to the server) to analyze; it would thereby save 99 percent of its costs (if it knew what the server did). If the server knows enough in advance, it can conclude that only one route out of the million provided is consistent with its *a priori* knowledge of the client's route (although there might have been another thousand routes that were also consistent, let us say that only one of them was in the million-route database). Revealing the route to the server would provide it information it did not possess—because the server had enough information to spot and ignore the phony data. The client also has to be careful that its true data do not stick out because the location is inherently interesting (e.g., the trip destination is an empty building) while few of the others are.

These tricks assume that information is subject to successive approximation (in the sense that acquiring small amounts of knowledge can cull the search space), but not all types of information have that character. They also assume that the cost of validating or acting on phony data is not trivial. The technique of hiding real values among phony values would not work with passwords when systems allow limitless guesses. But it may work quite well if the data could not be verified directly, and especially where the value of the right data consists in refining a judgment (e.g., how likely are they to strike here) rather than solving a puzzle.

For the final case, two or more entities would carry out a joint computation without having to reveal the data to each other. Although the most obvious alternative to using PROCEED technologies is to find someone who is trustworthy to all, doing so may be complex. Defining "trustworthy" may not necessarily be up to the parties involved. The data may be legally protected in ways that assume that no third party is trustworthy—but (see below) the same legal restrictions may not allow for SMP either. As a practical matter, the likelihood that one data holder will not accept a specific third party as trustworthy rises with the number of data holders whose permission is needed. In such cases, a relevant trade-off is between doing the computation with partial data vis-à-vis paying the computational/networking cost associated with using secure multiparty computation. When multiple parties need to concur, the relevant metric for the *value* of being able to use PROCEED technologies may *not* be the objective gain to each participant from avoiding the harm of disclosure (i.e., the likelihood that the possession of the data in unauthorized hands could lead to a greater likelihood of harmful decisions). Instead, it may be the likelihood that the most fearful of them would balk at releasing its data at all, hence preventing the computation.[23] Trust judgments must cover both peers (the authenticity of data is a problem irrespective of whether or not encryption is used) and computational providers. Trust could be measured objectively by understanding what motive someone has for looking at the data: What would the trusted parties gain from seeing the data; how susceptible are the trusted parties to the bribes, threats, or charm of others; and can the trusted parties be convinced that violations of trust can be detected and punished? Trust also tends to be measured subjectively and is influenced by personal factors: accidents of someone's history, institutional motivations (e.g., what is the cost of erring on the side of caution vis-à-vis sharing?), and the degree of merited confidence in one's ability to rate another person's trustworthiness.

In addition, similar psychological factors may inhibit potential participants from believing what mathematicians can verify—that their data will be secure even while permitting accurate computations

---

[23] If there were, for instance, a series of pairwise computations, multiple trusted parties could be used as long as every pair can identify one party that is trusted by both. If the computations require the participation of *all* parties, the odds of finding one party trusted by all decrease significantly.

to be carried out. Is it realistic to assume that they will be subjective (that is, overly fearful) about the cost to them of the risk (albeit small if the trustworthy party is truly trustworthy) of losing the confidentiality of their data but objective about evaluating the claims of mathematicians that their data will be safe?

A variant on finding someone trustworthy is to find some*thing* trustworthy. Imagine a standalone machine with its operating system and its algorithms in hardware. Two participants enter their unencrypted data using physical media (e.g., on USB sticks) whose data are then wiped (so that no conspiracy between one party and the machine pulls data from the other party). The computation is carried out; the results are returned in physical form (e.g., a printout) that can be verified to have no other data on it. The machinery's memory is wiped. The entire mechanism presumes that both parties can satisfy themselves through physical inspection (or by trusting experts' inspections) that their data have been wiped and at no time transferred to the other party. This model does require a dedicated machine and physical presence to generate the requisite trust—and its applicability is therefore limited when the parties cannot physically meet. A version in which the data are transferred remotely has many more places where data can pass beyond scrutiny and would likely be less psychologically satisfying, hence less workable.

Context removal. Yet another approach to reducing the risk of disclosure from processing encrypted data without paying a processing penalty is to remove the context from the data, leaving it as a set of numbers to be computed on. Such confidentiality strategies move and compute data in the clear but encrypt only when adding the metadata.

Such a strategy has a number of key prerequisites. Context removal has to be thorough. That can often mean removing not only the metadata but also indications of who owns the data. There are several approaches for the latter. One is to use a trusted cut-out whose link with the owner can be neither ascertained nor reasonably guessed. Another is to use quasi-cryptographic channels to move the information—e.g., Tor for moving data and some digital currency to pay for data services.

But decontexualization is not always applicable everywhere. To take a trivial example, if the data is a picture of a person's face, simply removing the name from the picture will not protect the data. More broadly, while data as numbers may *prima facie* be relatively context-free, data as audio, video, imagery, or maps tend to have inherent context. Similarly, removing a name from a record does not protect information if there are other data in the record (e.g., birth date, gender, ZIP code) that can collectively point to a particular individual.[24] As a practical matter, if context removal is to be more than a *pro forma* exercise, it may have to be red-teamed—an expense that may exceed the computational cost of using PROCEED technologies in the first place.

And even then the data may not be safe. If the data are presented as a data stream and some of the data track something observable (e.g., daily temperatures), a shrewd observer may be able to infer what the other data represent. Conversely, a combination of context removal and data multiplication may suffice to reduce the likelihood of a correct guess down to levels that do not give other parties the confidence to make or change their decisions. More generally, anonymizing data is notoriously difficult if the goal is to keep information secret from those who know the context behind the data.[25]

Other approaches to data-hiding: It is possible to avoid the computational penalties associated with PROCEED if the metadata were hidden and the data were structured so that there was a function, G(), that obeys the property that

- Fn (a,b) = Fn (G(a), G(b)).

---

[24] It was found that 87 percent (216 million out of 248 million) of the population in the United States had reported characteristics that likely made them unique based only on five-digit ZIP code, gender, and date of birth (Latanya Sweeney, "Simple Demographics Often Identify People Uniquely," Pittsburgh, Penn.: Carnegie Mellon University, Data Privacy Working Paper 3, 2000).

[25] See, for example, Sweeney (2000). A good discussion of the problems involved can also be found in Andrew Chin and Anne Klinefelter, "Differential Privacy as a Response to the Re-Identification Threat: The Facebook Advertiser Case Study," *North Carolina Law Review*, Vol. 90, No. 5, 2012.

- The parameters of G() can be hidden (weaker condition), or the parameters of G() can be hidden even if one knows b and G(b) (stronger condition).
- Knowing G(a) would not reveal a.

Another approach for computation if the point is to get a binary answer with very high degrees of likelihood or an analog answer up to a certain precision is to run a process similar to that of a zero-knowledge proof. For instance, in the millionaire problem, two parties can divide their wealth into a number of small categories with some random component. A probe that compares one party's component to another's a sufficient number of times can ascertain that one party is likely wealthier than another—if both sides are willing to allow a certain degree of ambiguity in the precision and certainty of the result and the components are relatively well behaved (e.g., one side has not put most of its assets into one category, which if not sampled can lead to the conclusion that this one side is less wealthy). In this case, there is a trade-off: The higher the desired confidence level, the closer one side will come to know what the other side's wealth is relative to its own (the closer each side's wealth is to one another, the sharper the dilemma, as well).

Again, only some problems are amenable to such treatment.

Conclusions

Unless and until the processing penalty for using PROCEED technologies shrinks well below 10^7, the decision to use them is likely to be a close one and thus may be influenced by many other factors that can push one toward or away from doing so. As noted, those who use PROCEED must be able to make subtle trust distinctions: too little, and there is no interoperation altogether; too much, and there is no need for hiding the data. Furthermore, if the data to be processed meet certain criteria, there may be alternative ways of preserving the equities of data holders (in minimizing the expected impact of disclosure) without undergoing such processing cost penalties.

Because the decision to use PROCEED technologies is expected to be a close one, other factors (e.g., government-imposed rules) have the potential to bias the amount of use in large ways. By contrast, for technologies where the case for or against use is easy to make given the particular circumstances of use (e.g., the decision to use Tor for someone wanting Internet access for political activity in repressive states vis-à-vis someone wanting real-time streaming in benevolent states), these other factors may hold less sway.

CHAPTER THREE

Trust and Environments in Russia and China

As noted in the previous chapter, trust plays a double-edged role in the uptake of PROCEED technologies: We encrypt because we do not trust others, but if we had zero trust in others we would not have the sort of business relationships that resulted in putting our data in their care in the first place. Investment in PROCEED technologies is influenced by trust because of asymmetries of information and conflicting preferences that arise when one party shares data with another and in so doing may prompt the moral hazard problem—i.e., the situation when a trusted party fails to protect data properly. This chapter first provides a theoretical framework for understanding the link between trust and the uptake of PROCEED technologies and then examines the interplay between trust and encryption in Russia and China, the two large countries with an appetite for technology, moderate levels of affluence, and competition that is an important concern to the U.S. Department of Defense. We compare these two countries to capture how histories, cultures, and political systems that are distinct from those of the West influence micro-level behavior when it comes to information security.

The amount of trust depends on situation, culture, and history. One person's trust toward another, first of all, depends on the parameters of a particular situation, from which rational calculations can be made. What is to be gained by trusting another? What can be lost? How does another stand to gain by violating one's trust; how does that party stand to lose? What track record does that party have? What is that party's track record in a particular situation? These decisions are driven by strategic considerations, and different people in the same situation should make the same trust decisions (as long as they have the same relationship or lack thereof with the trusted party).

Trust also reflects a person's or organization's history (and personality). In similar circumstances, different people will make different judgments about whether they can trust another party not to do something they do not want done. In certain circumstances, trust policies reflect an organizational consensus or are built into an organization's culture (that people then look to when making decisions) or are set down in an organization's policy. Such organizations could be public or private. The mechanisms are analogous.

Neither of these two types of trust factors would necessarily differentiate decisions made in the United States from those of Russia or China. Therefore, we look at cultural aspects of trust, which *are* strongly correlated with country. As argued by Frank Fukuyama[1] and observed by many others, some cultures are more likely to trust nonrelatives than other cultures do. High degrees of trust facilitate the construction of efficient organizations and the extension of debt (without onerous guarantees or collateral). Low degrees of trust tend to be associated with the formation of sole-proprietor or family-centric businesses.

Finally, trust reflects the legal and institutional context in which the transaction is executed. A U.S. firm might have to use encryption because it believes that it can exercise its rights not to give personal information to the government.[2] A Chinese firm would understand that it has no basis for denying information to the government.

To understand the differences that national cultures and circumstances make in the uptake of PROCEED technologies, we will look broadly at the nature of trust, and then discuss Russia and China in the context of what we have found.

---

[1] Francis Fukuyama, *Trust: The Social Virtues and the Creation of Prosperity*, New York, NY: Free Press, 1995.

[2] The unexpectedly robust use of national-security letters asking for broad-scale data access, however, means that such assurance may not be warranted when storing information on servers owned by others—unless the data owner encrypts its own data (and the encryption method is not tampered with) and holds the key.

The Role of Trust in Economic Transactions

Trust affects the uptake of the PROCEED technologies via two mechanisms: the moral hazard problem and the perception of cyber threat. We consider each of these channels in turn. The moral hazard problem is ubiquitous to many applied computer science problems that entail sharing sensitive information between the two parties—e.g., third-party encryption key management schemes, cloud computing services, PayPal transactions, intrusion detection systems, and file-sharing sites. In all these cases one party (the principal) transfers the control over information to the agent in exchange for receiving a service. Such transactions are prone to the principal-agent problem when (1) transacting parties have heterogeneous preferences about the level of effort required to achieve a specific outcome, (2) the principal cannot observe the level of effort exhorted by an agent, and (3) the agent has relatively more information than the principal about the state of the world. For instance, a party that shares its data with a cloud service provider has no knowledge of the security measures that the provider has in place to prevent unauthorized access to information and may not be even informed by the provider about any security breaches.[3] Cloud servers' preferences are determined by profit maximization considerations, and as markets for cloud services become more competitive and profit margins slimmer, providers may cut down on the security investment.[4]

Trust mitigates the moral hazard problem by creating an expectation that both sides will fulfill their duties even without prior agreement on all details of compensation.[5] As Ensminger notes, "[T]rust occurs neither randomly nor prematurely. It occurs in direct mea-

---

[3] Anya Kim and Ira S. Moskowitz, "Incentivized Cloud Computing: A Principal Agent Solution to the Cloud Computing Dilemma," Naval Research Laboratory Report # NRL/MR/5540-10-9292, September 15, 2010.

[4] Rico Knapper, Benjamin Blau, Tobias Conte, Anca Sailer, Andrzej Kochut, and Ajay Mohindra, "Efficient Contracting in Cloud Service Markets with Asymmetric Information—A Screening Approach," 2011 IEEE Conference on Commerce and Enterprise Computing, Luxembourg, Luxembourg, September 5–7, 2011, pp. 236–243.

[5] Ramon Casadesus-Masanell and Daniel F. Spulber, "Trust and Incentives in Agency," *South California Interdisciplinary Law Journal*, Vol. 15, No. 1, Fall 2005, pp. 45–104, p. 98.

sure to decreasing risk of the probability of cheating on the parts of both the principal and the agent, and this assessment is based on their incentives for long-term cooperation, their reputations, and the general social context of norm enforcement."[6] Spelling out such details becomes infeasible when the number of relevant contingencies exceeds what can be spelled out explicitly[7] or when the agent is entrusted with multiple tasks or serves multiple principles.[8] Trust works most effectively when both sides understand what constitutes a reasonably good performance under given circumstances and how performance is compensated. It allows formal contracts to be replaced by implicit expectation of a fair reward in exchange for good performance. The notion of fair pay and good effort emerges from practices accepted by the community to which both the principal and the agent both belong.[9]

As Casadesus-Masanell and Spulber note, trust between the principal and the agent is promoted through social norms, legal duties, and market standards, with each of them creating an alternative *ex post* enforcement mechanism in cases when explicit incentives cannot be fully spelled out *ex ante* (see Table 3.1). Social norms deter the agent from shirking and the principal from behaving opportunistically by creating a system of shared rules on what constitutes appropriate or inappropriate behavior—such as honesty, loyalty, and a good work ethic. To the extent that individuals are embedded in social networks, violation of these norms results in social pressure that may adversely affect their social status. Such norms induce optimum performance by ensuring that parties have proper incentives to perform even in the absence of explicit incentives, such as bonuses or commissions. Norms

---

[6] Jean Ensminger, "Reputations, Trust, and the Principal Agent Problem," in Karen S. Cook, ed., *Trust in Society*, New York, NY: Russell Sage Foundation, 2001, p. 199.

[7] Ensminger, 2001; Nabil I. Al-Najjar and Ramon Casadesus-Masanell, "Trust and Discretion in Agency Contracts," Harvard Business School Working Paper, April 2002. The authors show that in the situations with infinitely many factors affecting outcome, a principal's trustworthiness allows incomplete contracts to substitute for incomplete ones. Trustworthiness protects the agents from opportunistic behavior by the principal and makes the agent more likely to agree on incomplete contract.

[8] Casadesus-Masanell and Spulber, 2005.

[9] Casadesus-Masanell and Spulber, 2005, p. 47.

enhance efficiency because they reduce the amount of risk that should be shifted from the principal to the agent and by allowing the agent to be compensated in the form of flat payments rather than through a pay scheme contingent on the final output. Social norms also reduce the transaction cost of delegation by reducing the need or complexity of explicit contracts.[10]

Legal duties, which work by different mechanisms, are feasible only when the notion of fiduciary duties is imbedded in laws that impose penalties for breaching them. English common law requires agents to exercise care and skill in representing the principal's interests, to accurately report information to the principal, and to be loyal to the principal. These duties can be enforced in courts even if no contract spells them out. Legal penalties discourage the agent from shirking by reducing the size of agent's payoff if the contract is poorly executed.[11]

Markets help deter shirking when agent misbehavior is observable but cannot be enforced in courts because evidence is rarely good enough. Market standards emerge from repeated interactions among the same parties who provide a pool from which potential agents can be recruited—e.g., bar associations and professional associations. Parties in these networks share similar expertise with agents and, thus, can assess their professional performance even when the principal cannot monitor the agent. The most common sanction that these networks can use is to expel agents from the network—a particularly effective deterrent for agents with lengthy time horizons.[12]

The roles of contracts, peer groups, courts, and markets are summarized in Table 3.1.

Observational and experimental studies, notably of financial transactions, confirm that trust facilitates delegation and reduces perceived risk of moral hazard. Howorth and Moro[13] show that small businesses in northern Italy pay lower interest rates on overdraft loans when

---

[10] Casadesus-Masanell and Spulber, 2005, pp. 56–60.

[11] Casadesus-Masanell and Spulber, 2005, pp. 60–65.

[12] Casadesus-Masanell and Spulber, 2005, pp. 74–85.

[13] Carole Howorth and Andrea Moro, "Trustworthiness and Interest Rates: An Empirical Study of Italian SMEs," *Small Business Economics*, Vol. 39, 2012, pp. 161–177.

Table 3.1
How Trust Can Improve Delegation

	Incentives for Performance	Trust	Transaction Costs
Contract	Rewards/penalties based on performance	Strict reliance on contract terms assumes absence of trust	High transaction costs of writing/monitoring complete contracts
Social context	Violating norms affects social status and conscience	Trust established by social pressures and personal ethics	Transaction costs lowered by social norms; incomplete contracts
Legal context	Penalties for breaches of duty and/or trust	Agent is fiduciary; law defines a trust relationship	Transaction costs lowered because of law of agency
Market context	Penalties based on reputation, future transactions, access to market networks	Trust established by reputation and informal market networks	Transaction costs lowered because of market standards; implicit contracts

SOURCE: Casadesus-Masanell and Spulber, 2005.

bankers perceived them as trustworthy—as measured by a lender's competence, responsiveness to clients' needs, and honesty in negotiations with commercial partners. Such information cannot be conveyed through financial statements, which frequently understate true profits for tax reasons. Bank managers' perception of borrowers' trustworthiness emerges from the information shared by clients and businesses and overall reputation of business owners in the community.[14] Guiso et al.[15] further show that trust and social capital influence households' asset allocation and firms' access to credit, hence the development of the financial sector. Those who live in neighborhoods with high levels of social capital and trust put more of their wealth into the bank; those who live in low-trust areas hoard cash. Where social capital is high, sellers are more likely to trust that the checks they get will not bounce.

---

[14] Howorth and Moro, 2012, pp. 173–174.

[15] Luigo Guiso, Paola Sapienza, and Luigi Zingales, "The Role of Social Capital in Financial Development," National Bureau of Economic Research, Working Paper 7563, February 2000.

Such habits linger even after households move out of low-trust areas to high-trust areas. Trust is also positively correlated with the probability that a household will use checks and with the use of formal rather than informal markets (households from low-trust areas borrow from family and friends, not banks). Similarly, firms in low-trust areas have fewer shareholders.

Experimental studies confirm that trust facilitates principal-agent interactions because agents shirk less and principals reward them more than principal-agent frameworks predict. In one lab experiment, although most MBA students failed to negotiate contacts that would induce high levels of effort, they still supplied high efforts even though others never found out about their behavior. In another, participants transferred more of their profits to others when they perceived those others as more trustworthy. In a third, employees who received prior compensation based on expectations that they would work hard did not shirk even though the employer could not punish them afterwards.[16]

From the principal-agent framework, economic actors will switch to the PROCEED technologies when they cannot find a trusted third party for performing services needed on the sensitive data. When social and legal channels for addressing the moral hazard problem are dysfunctional and the overall level of trust among economic actors is low, transacting parties will use the PROCEED technologies to minimize their vulnerability to the moral hazard problem in exchange for additional processing and economic costs. Data encryption using PROCEED technologies slows down computations by 10^7, and in so doing increases the cost of protecting data. Uptake of PROCEED technologies then becomes rational when parties cannot induce the agent not to behave opportunistically.

Trust can also affect the demand for PROCEED technologies via the perception of cyber threat. Like any other form of information security investment, PROCEED technologies impose economic costs. Economic actors' willingness to pay for those costs will depend on the

---

[16] Gary J. Miller and Andrew B. Whitford, "Trust and Incentives in Principal-Agent Negotiations—The 'Insurance/Incentive Trade-Off,'" *Journal of Theoretical Politics*, Vol. 14, No. 2, 2002, pp. 231–267.

probability of unauthorized access to proprietary data, especially while they are being decrypted to allow the third party to perform computations. Factors that affect a firm's investment in information security have been examined in depth by other scholars and include vulnerability of information to unauthorized access, investment levels of other actors in the network, extent of positive externalities in the network, availability of private insurance, and the underlying beliefs about types of hackers.[17] Generally, when left on their own, economic actors underinvest in information security either because they perceive information security as an outcome of collective effort by all actors in a network and expect payoffs to be determined by the security of the weakest link in the network, or because actors who store and process sensitive information are not the ones who bear losses as a result of unauthorized access.[18]

Both game theoretic and decisionmaking approaches suggest that economic actors invest in information security more when they assign a higher probability to a cyber attack.[19] Experimental evidence from cognitive psychology suggests that individuals assign these probabilities based on emotional attitudes, culture, and trust. Perceived risk is

---

[17] Lawrence A. Gordon and Martin P. Loeb, "The Economics of Information Security Investment," *ACM Transactions on Information and System Security*, Vol. 5, No. 4, November 2002, pp. 438–457; Kjell Hausken, "Returns to Information Security Investment: The Effect of Alternative Information Security Breach Functions on Optimal Investment and Sensitivity to Vulnerability," *Information System Frontiers*, Vol. 8, No. 5, December 2006; Daron Acemoglu, Azarakhsh Malekian, and Asu Ozdaglar, "Network Security and Contagion," NBER Working Paper No. 19174, June 18, 2013; Jens Grossklags, Nicolas Christin, and John Chuang, "Secure or Insure? A Game-Theoretic Analysis of Information Security Games," WWW 2008, April 21–22, 2008; Huseyin Cavusoglu, Srinivasan Raghunathan, and Wei T. Yue, "Decision-Theoretic and Game-Theoretic Approaches to IT Security Investment," *Journal of Management Information Systems*, Vol. 25, No. 2, Fall 2008, pp. 281–304.

[18] Ross Anderson, "Why Information Security Is Hard: An Economic Perspective," Proceedings of the 17th Annual Computer Security Applications Conference, December 10–14, 2001; Ross Anderson and Tyler Moore, "The Economics of Information Security," *Science*, Vol. 314, October 27, 2006.

[19] See, in particular, Gordon and Loeb (2002) and Cavusoglu, Raghunathan, and Yue (2008).

higher when individuals have lower levels of trust that others are competent enough to perform complex tasks.[20]

Implications of Trust for PROCEED-Based Encryption and Other Forms of Encryption

Cross-country and cross-community differences in the level of trust can influence the uptake of PROCEED technologies by affecting the perception of how a service provider will handle the data and by altering the perception of cyber threat (Figure 3.1). Low levels of trust discourage economic actors from entering any types of transactions, and

Figure 3.1
The Relationship Between Trust and Demand for PROCEED Technologies

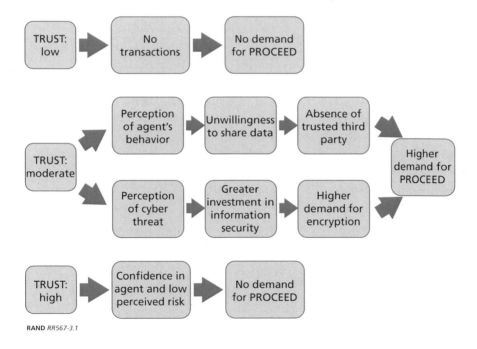

RAND RR567-3.1

---

[20] Jonathan Jackson, Nick Allum, and George Gaskell, "Perceptions of Risk in Cyberspace," in Robin Mansell and Brian S. Collins, eds., *Trust and Crime in Information Societies*, Cheltenham, UK: Edward Elgar, 2005, pp. 245–281.

thus there will be no demand for the PROCEED technologies because parties do not perceive cooperation to be mutually beneficial whether it is enabled by the PROCEED technologies or not. At the moderate level of trust, cooperation becomes mutually beneficial; however, the party that owns information is concerned with the moral hazard problem. This increases the demand for the PROCEED technologies because they eliminate the need for the trusted third party to perform computation on unencrypted data. Perception of risk is the second reason why the demand for the PROCEED technologies will be relatively high in the environment with the moderate level of trust. Economic actors will accept economic and time costs imposed by PROCEED technologies when they expect a cyber attack to happen with a high probability. Perceived risk is inversely correlated with trust. Finally, the demand for encryption will be lower when the level of trust is very high and contracting parties trust each other well enough to share unencrypted data.

Empirical Evidence from Russia and China

The goal of the empirical analysis is to examine whether theoretical discussion is consistent with observational data. Ideally, one would like to have survey data on economic actors' perception of the potential value of the PROCEED technologies for doing business. However, collection of these data are not feasible either in Russia or China. Fortunately, there are publicly available national representative surveys on the level of trust in these populations for both of these countries. We therefore combined these survey data with online search trends about encryption and information security to estimate how trust affects population interest in (1) data encryption, (2) information security, and (3) data protection. We expect that the demand for encryption technologies, including the PROCEED ones, will be correlated with the demand for information about them. We will use these data to test for possible trust-encryption linkages.

Trust and Information Security in Russia

Russia's market for encryption in 2012 comprised $556 million and is expected to reach $866 million by 2016.[21] The largest domestic suppliers of information security and data protection are Kaspersky Lab (2,000 employees), Akronis (430 employees), and R-Style (160 employees). Cisco is the major foreign supplier. Moscow constitutes the prime location for information security firms.[22] Before 2011, the demand for information security products came primarily from the government and large investment and insurance companies because they dealt with the clients and employees who frequently accessed sensitive information remotely, including via mobile phones and iPads.[23] The demand for information security products elsewhere has lagged but is catching up (Figure 3.2). In spite of these developments, the majority of Russians still believe that their personal data are not adequately protected by private and public organizations.[24]

The Russian government has been behind the expansion of the information security markets. It perceives data protection as an issue of national security,[25] and in 2012 it made commercial and government entities liable for failing to secure personal information provided by their customers and imposed mandatory data encryption requirements. Markets for encryption technologies subsequently swelled.[26]

These markets are tightly regulated by the Russian authorities, who impose licensing and key-sharing requirements. Enterprises must

---

[21] CyberSecurity.ru, "Объем Рынка Шифрования Данных Удвоится В Предстоящие 5 Лет" ["The Russian Encryption Market Will Double in 5 Years"], April 12, 2013.

[22] CNews Analytics, "Крупнейшие ИТ-компании России в сфере защиты информации" ["Largest IT Companies in Russia in the Area of Protection of Personal Data"], 2011.

[23] TOPS Business Integrator, "Аналитика рынка ИБ в России 2010–2011 гг" ["Analysis of IT Security Market in Russia 2010–2011"], undated.

[24] FOM, "Защита персональных данных" ["Protection of Personal Data"], May 13, 2013.

[25] "Доктрина информационной безопасности Российской Федерации" ["Information Security Doctrine of the Russian Federation"], *Rossiyskaya Gazeta*, undated.

[26] Cambridge Advocate Legal News Services, "The Law on Liability for Violation of the Law on the Protection of Personal Data Came Into Effect," Newswire, July 24, 2011.

Figure 3.2
Information Security Consumers

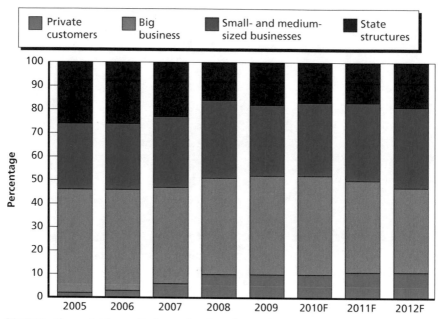

SOURCE: Alexandr Vlasov, "Information Security Market in Russia Keeps Growing in Spite of the Crisis," Groteck Business Media, Global Security Mag, August 2010.
RAND RR567-3.2

obtain licenses in order to develop, disseminate, and maintain encryption facilities, as well as to provide any other data encryption services. To be approved by the authorities, encryption algorithms should be symmetric and should follow the GOST 28147-89 algorithm (which was developed in 1990 and used in the post-Soviet space). GOST has a 64-bit block size and a key length of 256 bits. The law enforcement authorities have unlimited access to the keys used for encryption.[27] Licenses are also required for importing most encryption technologies. Only products developed for mass consumption that have built-in encryption, such as tokens, personal credit cards with microchips,

---

[27] "Russian Laws and Regulations: Implications for Kaspersky Labs," *Wired*, February 2013; BSA, "Global Cloud Computing Scorecard: Russia," 2013.

mobile phones, ATM machines, and so on, are exempt. Fines for using unlicensed encryption technologies are regulated by the same law that regulates the use of other unlicensed IT products.

To estimate the link between Russia's population's demand for information security and trust, we focus on the frequency of online search queries submitted from Russia in Russian for the following keywords: *"shifrovaniye dannykh"* ["data encryption"], *"zashchita dannykh"* ["data protection"], and *"informatzionnaya bezopastnost"* ["information security"]. These terms, although related, encompass somewhat different concepts. Both data protection and information security regulate sharing personal data, in both electronic and nonelectronic formats. Information security and IT security (*IT-bezopastnost*) are used interchangeably in Russian sources, but information security has a higher search volume. Data encryption refers to electronic data only. We selected this combination of terms based on high rates of intercorrelation in the Yandex.ru search results. Using more than one construct maximizes the external validity of our analysis.

Although multiple search engines are available in Russia, we used queries submitted to the Yandex search engine because it has the largest market share; it is frequently referred to as "the Google of Russia."[28] Yandex.ru reports statistics on the popularity of search queries. Ideally we would like to have the data that cover the period 2007–2013, but Yandex.ru provides historical data only for the past 24 months.[29]

The number of queries for encryption, as shown in Figure 3.3, was much lower than for the two other key words, which suggests that encryption is still a rather novel concept for many Russian Internet users and thus that they may not be ready to pay a premium to keep those who process their data from looking at it. The frequency of searches varies by region. Interest in "data encryption" is the highest for the northwest (i.e., the St. Petersburg area), whereas the interest

---

[28] Jordan Robertson, "Why Google Isn't Winning in Russia," *Global Tech*, April 26, 2013; Hitmeter.ru, *"Reyting Uspol'zuyemikh Poiskovikh System v Dekabre 2012"* ["Ranking of the Most Popular Search Engines"], undated; Anna Makarova, "Poiskoviye Systemy Runeta" ["RuNet Search Engines"], in *Internet v Rossii* [*Internet in Russia*], Russian Association for Electronic Communications, June 2012.

[29] Yandex.ru, wordstat.yandex.ru, keyword search stats, undated.

Figure 3.3
Yandex Search Queries, 2011–2013

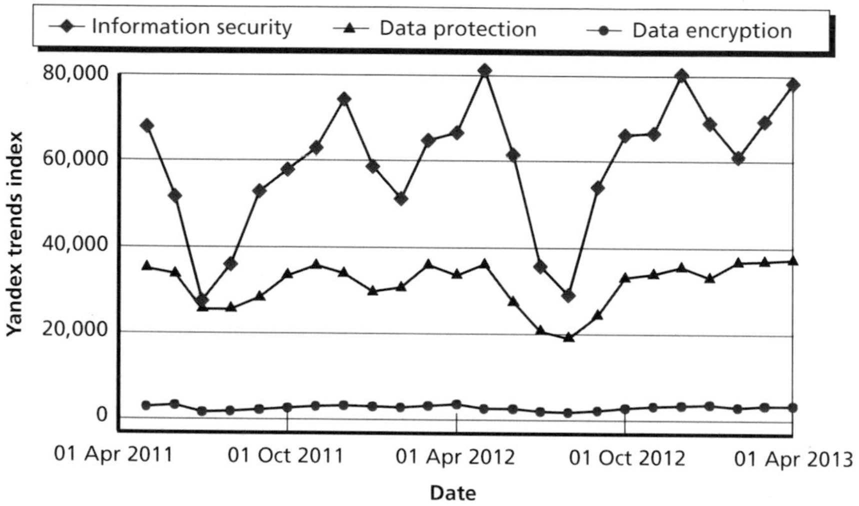

SOURCE: Compiled from http://wordstat.yandex.ru (Yandex.ru, undated).
RAND RR567-3.3

in "information security" and "data protection" is the highest for far Siberia.

We then tested for correlations between popular interest in data encryption, data protection, and information security on the one hand and trust on the other. Our data on trust come from the *Monitoring of Socio-Economic Changes* survey conducted in 2008 in 56 out of 83 regions by the Foundation for Monitoring of Public Opinion (FOM). The survey is one of the major national representative surveys and has been conducted quarterly since 1993. The most recent wave that contains questions about trust dates back to 2008. For our analysis, we focused on three types of trust: (1) interpersonal trust, (2) trust toward the government, and (3) trust toward law enforcement agencies. Since the goal of our analysis is to conduct a systematic comparison between Russia and China, we had to use surveys that had similar questions for both countries.[30] We computed, for each such region, the percentage of respondents who strongly agreed with the following statements: "The government can be trusted," "Police and courts can be trusted," and "The majority of people can be trusted." We also controlled for the level of regional development and the percentage of the respondents employed in a public sector.[31]

Table 3.2 reports the estimated coefficients from linear models with the relative frequency of queries as dependent variables. Relative frequency measures the number of queries for the specific keyword submitted from each region in Russia adjusted for overall number of search queries submitted from this region. Looking at the relative rather than absolute number of queries accounts for cross-regional variation in web traffic to the specific search engine. Each coefficient represents change in the frequency of queries as a result of a unit change in an independent variable, while holding all other values constant.

Low levels of trust toward the government and law enforcement officials are the key drivers of interest in data protection and information security. A 1-percentage-point increase in the share of the population that strongly agrees that the government can be trusted is associated, respectively, with a 2.8-percentage-point decrease in the frequency of queries about data protection and with a 1.73-percentage-point decrease in interest in information security (columns 5 and 8). Similarly, a 1-percentage-point increase in the share of people who trust police is associated with about a 4-percentage-point reduction in interest in data protection and a 2.3-percentage-point reduction in interest in information security (columns 6 and 9). The coefficients on the interpersonal trust variable are also negative but are not statistically significant, which suggests that interpersonal trust does not have any

---

[30] Questions for the Russia survey are as follows: (1) "In your opinion, generally speaking can people be trusted or should one be very careful when dealing with others?" (2) "How much do you trust the Russian Duma?" (3) "To what extent do you trust courts and law enforcement officials?" (FOM, 2008).

[31] The percentage of people employed in the public sector was constructed from the occupational background of respondents included in the *Monitoring of Socio-Economic Changes Survey* (FOM, 2008). The gross domestic product (GDP) figures come from *Regiony Rossii* published annually by the Russian Statistical Agency Goskomstat (2008).

Table 3.2
Estimated Coefficients of the Effects of Trust on Yandex Search Queries, Russia, 2011–2013

	Data Encryption			Data Protection			Information Security		
	(1)	(2)	(3)	(4)	(5)	(6)	(7)	(8)	(9)
Trust people	−0.12			−1.56			−0.51		
	(0.65)			(1.02)			(0.37)		
Trust government		1.81			−2.80[a]			−1.73[a]	
		(2.23)			(1.61)			(1.01)	
Trust police			−1.21			−4.04[b]			−2.37[b]
			(2.09)			(1.73)			(1.05)
% in public sector	−0.08	0.07	−0.11	1.06[a]	1.06[a]	1.10[a]	0.04	−0.02	0.01
	(0.76)	(0.72)	(0.72)	(0.59)	(0.61)	(0.63)	(0.28)	(0.27)	(0.26)
Avg. GDP/ capita 2008–2013	−0.00	0.00	−0.00	−0.00	−0.00	−0.00	0.00[b]	0.00	0.00
	(0.00)	(0.00)	(0.00)	(0.00)	(0.00)	(0.00)	(0.00)	(0.00)	(0.00)
Constant	103.27[b]	88.34[b]	107.04[c]	99.48[c]	88.96[c]	89.69[c]	114.74[c]	117.10[c]	116.90[c]
	(41.08)	(34.65)	(34.06)	(26.51)	(27.20)	(27.25)	(19.49)	(16.86)	(16.57)
Observations	54	54	54	56	56	56	56	56	56
R-squared	0.00	0.01	0.00	0.11	0.08	0.10	0.05	0.06	0.09

NOTE: Robust standard errors are in parentheses.
[a] $p < 0.1$.
[b] $p < 0.05$.
[c] $p < 0.01$.

effect on the demand for information about information security or data protection (columns 4 and 7).

The results for data encryption are weaker: Although the coefficients are negative in two out of three cases (columns 1 and 3), they are smaller in magnitude and are not statistically significant. This might be due to the fact that for Russian Internet users encryption is much more of a novel concept than the two other terms. It is also highly likely that technology enthusiasts submit the largest share of queries about encryption. These people adopt new technologies for the sake of experimentation. Most consumers, though, are motivated primarily by pragmatism.[32] Table 3.2 suggests that when it comes to data protection products, trust matters more to mass consumers than to early adopters.

Trust and Information Security in China

Chinese demand for data encryption has been driven mostly by hundreds of millions of dollars worth of government procurement, as well as by the finance and telecommunication sectors.[33] New legislation has also pushed demand forward; in 2007, the Chinese Ministry of Public Security issued a new regulatory policy[34] requiring Chinese banking/financing industries, government-owned research institutes, and defense manufacturers to implement data protection procedures that strictly conform with China's data protection protocols and standards. This was strengthened by a 2009 amendment[35] (Amendment 7 of the PRC Criminal Law) on data protection, which especially applied to those involved in government procurement, finance, and telecommunications. The amendment stipulated that employees who leak data from government organizations, as well as financial, telecommunication, and other data-sensitive sectors, could be imprisoned for up to ten years. For these reasons, the Chinese data encryption market demand (notably software encryption) increased by 50 percent annually

---

[32] Geoffrey A. Moore, *Crossing the Chasm: Marketing and Selling Disruptive Products to Mainstream Customers*, New York, NY: Harper Collins Books, 1991.

[33] Loretta Chao, "Beijing to Impose Encryption Disclosure Rules," *Wall Street Journal*, April 29, 2010.

[34] The Ministry of Public Safety of People's Republic of China, "信息安全等级保护管理办法（公通字[2007]43号）" ["Information Security Protection Management Regulations, [2007] No. 43"], June 22, 2007.

[35] The Central People's Government of the People's Republic of China, "中华人民共和国刑法修正案" ["The 7th Amendment to the Criminal Law of the People's Republic of China"], February 28, 2009.

between 2007 and 2010. Most of the demand lies in software encryption. In 2009, China's data encryption market reached $50 million.[36]

Like Russia, China regulates encryption products. China's State Encryption Management Bureau mandates that vendors of imported technological products release the details of the encryption codes for censorship purposes;[37] such imports also require government licenses. Since PROCEED technologies often come with a great deal of proprietary methods (e.g., to turn normal algorithms into those that compute using circuits), the terms under which foreign vendors would sell into the Chinese market have yet to be determined. Unlike Russia, whose laws spell out which products are exempt from regulation, China's Regulations for the Administration of Commercial Encryption do not spell out the set of products to which the regulation applies; hence, the set of encryption products subject to licensing could be quite broad. This leaves the enforcement decision in the hands of law enforcement and customs officials, who frequently apply ad hoc standards.[38]

As we did with Russia, we measured the demand for information about data encryption in China by counting the number of search queries submitted from China in Mandarin for the following keywords: "数据加密" ["data encryption"], "数据保护" ["data protection"], and "信息安全" ["information security"]. In Chinese sources, IT security and information security are used interchangeably. We selected these three terms because of the high correlation in the volume of searches for each of them.

We used Google.com search trends rather than Baidu because the latter does not report historical search trends at the regional level that could be used for this analysis. Our period covers both the years when Google was still present in China and then had the second largest share of searches, and three years after Google decided to pull out

---

[36] Esai Technologies, "2009年中国加密软件行业大势" ["The Trends of Chinese Encryption Software Industry as of 2009"], blog post, 51CTO, January 31, 2010.

[37] Chao, 2010.

[38] Christopher Cloutier and Jane Y. Cohen, "Casting a Wide Net: China's Encryption Regulation," *WorldECR*, November 2011.

of China, which substantially lowered its current market share.[39] The data are shown in Figure 3.4. Data encryption and protection appeared on the agenda of Chinese Internet users after 2006; by 2013 the level of interest had reached the same level as it did for information security. The spike of searches for data protection in 2006 was prompted by two major events in that year. First, in early 2006, the state supreme legislation organization—the National People's Congress—deliberated over the proposed "personal information and data protection bill,"[40] which stimulated vibrant public debates about the pros and cons of the bill. Second, in late 2006, major provincial government and the military also launched programs to develop data protection technolo-

Figure 3.4
Google Search Trends, China 2006–2013

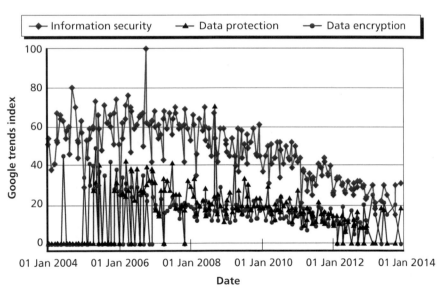

SOURCE: Constructed by the authors using Google search trends.
RAND RR567-3.4

---

[39] Kristina Wilson, Yaneli Ramos, and Daniel Harvey, "Google in China: The Great Firewall," The Kenan Institute for Ethics, Duke University, undated.

[40] Sina Tech, "关于出台《个人信息数据保护法》的提案" ["A Proposal: The Personal Information Protection and Data Protection Bill, Introduced by Democratic National Construction Association Central Committee Vice Chairman Chen Li"], March 8, 2006.

gies. Specifically, in October 2006, the Guangzhou military district launched a research program to develop data protection technologies to manage and protect classified data, protect smart networks, and guarantee safe formatting of data.[41] In December 2006, Guangdong province invested $100 million (¥600 million) to protect government data, including social security information and post-disaster data recovery.[42]

Another spike in the searches for data protection is observed immediately after an Amendment (Amendment No. 7) was added in February 2009 to the Criminal Law of the People's Republic of China to include a clause on personal information protection.[43] The amendment stipulated that five categories of entities (state government agencies, financial organizations, telecommunications companies, education providers, and medical service providers) are obliged to protect the personal information of Chinese citizens and that any individual affiliated with these entities who exposes, sells, or illegally provides citizen information to another party will face up to three years in prison.

We also disaggregated search queries by province. The interest in data encryption and protection is the highest in the more industrialized regions in the southeast, whereas the interest in information security is roughly the same across the country.

Self-reported trust indexes were computed from the most recent publicly available wave of the World Values Survey, administered in 2007 to the national representative sample of adults from all 23 of China's provinces. We focused on questions about interpersonal trust, as well as trust toward the government and police, measured by the overall level of confidence. Using geographic identifiers, we computed the percentage of respondents in each region who strongly agree that "the government can be trusted" and who have a great deal of confi-

---

[41] People's Liberty Army Daily, "广州军区研制涉密数据安全保护系统" ["Guangzhou Military District Conducts Research on Classified Data Protection System"], October 25, 2006.

[42] Southern News Industry Network, "粤拟投资六亿保护社保数据" ["Guangdong Province Plans to Invest ¥600 Million to Protect Social Security Data"], December 26, 2006.

[43] Xinhuanet, "刑法修正案草案　单位泄露公民个人信息将追究刑责" ["The Draft Amendment to the Criminal Law Unit Divulge Personal Information of Citizens Will Be Held Criminally Liable"], February 25, 2009.

dence in police or government.[44] To make the timing of the survey and Google search queries congruent, we restricted the data on Google search queries to the period 2007–2013. We also controlled for GDP per capita and the percentage of population employed in the public sector.[45]

Table 3.3 reports the estimated coefficients from the linear regression model, with the dependent variable being the frequency of queries for a specific keyword. The results show that the underlying mechanisms that contribute to the popular interest in the new technologies differ in China and Russia. In Russia, interest in data protection and information security is higher in regions with lower levels of trust toward the government and law enforcement officials. In China, interpersonal trust is the only statistically significant variable. The volume of search queries for encryption declines by 72 points and by 56 points for information security as the share of people with a high level of interpersonal trust increases by 1 percentage point (columns 1 and 7). The direction of correlation is also negative for the search volume for data protection, but the coefficient is statistically insignificant (column 4). The coefficients on the two other trust variables are statistically indistinguishable form zero in either of the model specifications.

These results suggest that there is a fundamental difference in how culture affects a population's demand for data protection and information security. If distrust toward state institutions is the primary driver in Russia, in China interpersonal trust is more important than trust toward the government.

---

[44] The questions were (1) "Generally speaking, would you say that most people can be trusted or that you need to be very careful in dealing with people?" (2) "I am going to name a number of organizations. For each one, could you tell me how much confidence you have in them: is it a great deal of confidence, quite a lot of confidence, not very much confidence or none at all? The Government." (3) "I am going to name a number of organizations. For each one, could you tell me how much confidence you have in them: is it a great deal of confidence, quite a lot of confidence, not very much confidence or none at all? The police."

[45] The percentage of people employed in the public sector was constructed from the occupational background of respondents included in the World Values Survey. The GDP figures come from the World Bank Economic Development Indicators (2013).

Table 3.3
Correlation Between Google Search Queries and Trust, China, 2007–2013

Variable	Encryption			Data Protection			Information Security		
	(1)	(2)	(3)	(4)	(5)	(6)	(7)	(8)	(9)
Trust people	-72.56^b			-32.26			-56.95^c		
	(28.30)			(25.27)			(19.31)		
Trust government		1.61			-10.49			13.02	
		(19.87)			(18.03)			(21.32)	
Trust police			1.61			-10.49			13.02
			(19.87)			(18.03)			(21.32)
% in public sector	25.39	29.48	29.48	-0.93	-0.60	-0.60	34.45^b	39.23^a	39.23^a
	(15.15)	(21.15)	(21.15)	(16.64)	(19.25)	(19.25)	(14.43)	(19.45)	(19.45)
GDP per capita	0.00^c	0.00^c	0.00^c	0.00^c	0.00^c	0.00^c	0.00^c	0.00^c	0.00^c
	(0.00)	(0.00)	(0.00)	(0.00)	(0.00)	(0.00)	(0.00)	(0.00)	(0.00)
Constant	5.08	-32.72^a	-32.72^a	2.22	-8.37	-8.37	-2.79	-38.98^b	-38.98^b
	(13.35)	(15.65)	(15.65)	(15.38)	(11.34)	(11.34)	(12.07)	(17.77)	(17.77)
Observations	21	21	21	21	21	21	21	21	21
R-squared	0.80	0.73	0.73	0.66	0.66	0.66	0.81	0.76	0.76

NOTE: Robust standard errors are in parentheses.
[a] $p < 0.1$.
[b] $p < 0.05$.
[c] $p < 0.01$.

PROCEED Technologies in Russia and China

What does this imply for the diffusion of PROCEED technologies in Russia and China? These results speak to the cross-country differences in the impact of trust in encryption, data protection, and information security. In Russia, cross-regional differences in search volume are driven by the perception of the state institutions; whereas in China, interpersonal trust is the key factor. We expect that the decision to uptake PROCEED technologies will also be influenced more by Chinese cross-regional differences in interpersonal trust, with provinces in which this trust is lower adopting PROCEED technologies faster, everything else holding equal, while the perception of the government will influence Russian demand for the PROCEED technologies.

Now we focus on the current level of interest in fully homomorphic encryption in Russia, China, and the United States. To begin with, many fewer Russians inquire about homomorphic encryption using search engines than do people in China or the United States (Figure 3.5). Currently, one page on the social media site www.habrahabr.ru is the major source of information about Craig Gentry's seminal work on homomorphic encryption and other relevant publications.[46]

This suggests that the demand for FHE in Russia is likely to remain weak, and even if it strengthens it may be limited by (1) when Russia's authorities decide to allow FHE, (2) when information security providers decide to recommend its use to Russian enterprises, and (3) how soon Russian consumers are willing to pay higher charges for FHE. The mass consumer demand for PROCEED will be affected by how much they trust the government and law enforcement officials.

Prior to 2012 there had been no serious interest in FHE among Chinese Internet users, but in 2012, the number of Google queries spiked and surpassed those in the United States and Russia. If (1) this trend persists in China, (2) China's authorities approve the use of PROCEED technologies, and (3) there are tech-savvy individuals who want the technology, the chances are higher than for Russia that there will be customers willing to pay the processing premium to use PROCEED technologies. The demand for the PROCEED technology will be higher in Chinese regions with lower levels of interpersonal trust.

---

[46] Habrahabr.ru, "Гомоморфное шифрование своими руками" ["Do It Yourself: Homomorphic Encryption"], blog post, August 23, 2012.

Figure 3.5
Searches for "Homomorphic Encryption"

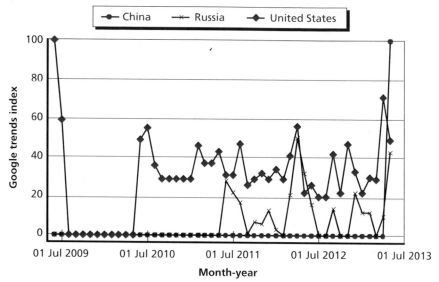

SOURCE: Google search trends. For Russia, we used Google search trends for "gomomrphniye shifrovaniya"; for China, we used "同态加密."
RAND RR567-3.5

Cloud Computing and PROCEED Technologies

The uptake of PROCEED technologies will be also affected by the expansion of cloud computing, and China currently outperforms Russia in the growth of this sector. The adoption of cloud computing in Russia began much later than in China, and Russia's cloud computing markets are currently significantly smaller than those in China (Table 3.4).

Russia

Infrastructure-as-a-Service (IaaS): The IaaS sector accounts for the largest share of Russia's cloud computing market. The sector is dominated by two Russia-based system integrators, I-Teco and Krok, which account respectively for 38 and 28 percent of the IaaS market, followed by ActivCloud, based in Belarus, which controls 22 percent

Table 3.4
Cloud Computing Market in Russia and China

	Russia		China	
	2012 (million USD)	**Projected Growth and Capitalization, 2017 (million USD)**	**2012 (million USD)**	**Projected Growth and Capitalization, 2017 (million USD)**
Infrastructure-as-a-service (IaaS)	$78.48	40% $247.97	$85.17 (511 million RMB)	50% (CAGR) $647.30
Software-as-a-service (SaaS)	$43.95	50% $307.58	$583 (3.5 billion RMB)	87.4% (CAGR) $13,460
Platform-as-a-service (PaaS)	$0.31	600% $21.9	$30.6 (184 million RMB)	87.4% (CAGR) $707
Total	$141.26	330%, $466,000	$698.77 (4.2 billion RMB)	$14,810

SOURCES: Oleg Sincha, "За 4 года рынок облачных услуг в РФ вырастет почти на 330%" ["Russia's Cloud Market Will Grow in 4 Times Over the Next 4 Years"], blog post summarizing Orange Business Survey Report, February 20, 2013; China Internet Network Information Center (CINIC), 中国互联网发展报告（2013）[*The 32nd China Internet Development Statistics Report, 2013*], July 2013.

NOTE: CAGR = compound annual growth rate; RMB = renminbi.

of the market. Current market capitalization is about $78 million, and the projected growth rate is about 40 percent.

The following factors have constrained the expansion of IaaS in Russia:

- Nontransparent pricing schemes, distrust of technology, and the lack of confidence that data would be protected.[47]
- There is considerable uncertainty about who has access to data stored on a cloud, especially when these clouds are outside Russia.

---

[47] J'son & Partners Consulting, "Российский рынок IaaS" ["Market Watch: Russian IaaS Market"], September 2013.

Because the regulatory framework is vague, Russian firms are hesitant to store data on the cloud.

- Technical and business reliability is an issue; it is common for servers to change the terms of services after a company migrates to the cloud.

- The primary potential customers, Russian banks (notably departments engaged in risk assessment and price forecasting), prefer "private clouds" that they own themselves because they do not trust cloud service providers not to disclose confidential and proprietary data to somebody else. They are willing only to entrust email and similarly inessential services to the cloud. The heads of the major banks reject the idea of switching to public cloud in the next five years because there is no guarantee that the servers will not disclose information to competitors. They also do not trust public service providers to provide computations in a timely manner. [48]

The *Software-as-a-Service (SaaS)* sector is just beginning to form in Russia, and its growth has been driven by investors' inflated expectations about returns on investment that led to the influx of start-up companies that expect a quick turnaround. The market is fragmented among multiple providers, and some of them provide SaaS for free because they have not yet developed ways of collecting tariffs. Some companies are operating at a loss. Industry experts identify piracy and the lack of confidence that SaaS infrastructure is reliable as the key obstacles to the expansion of the SaaS sector. The demand for SaaS is low in Russia because unlicensed copies of software are less expensive and mechanisms for enforcing intellectual property law do not exist. Large companies that can afford to pay for licensed software are reluc-

---

[48] See Andrey Beshkov, "Андрей Бешков: Безопасность в «облаке»" ["Andrey Beshkov: Safety in the "Cloud"], Cloudzone.ru, blog post, December 22, 2011; Oksana Dyachenko, "Банки присматриваются к «облакам»" ["Banks Are Looking at the "Cloud"], *National Bank Journal*, July 24, 2012; and Kosntantin Grashenko, "Бизнес обживает облака" ["Business Cloud Settles"], CRN, No. 3 (71), July 2, 2012.

tant to switch to SaaS because they lack confidence that service will not be interrupted by glitches in IT infrastructure.[49]

The *Platform-as-a-Service (PaaS)* sector is the least developed one. In 2012, it accounted for 2 percent of the entire cloud market because of the insufficient demand for this type of service among Russian enterprises.

Because cloud computing industry is still only in the nascent stages, the demand for performing computations on encrypted data by the third party is still very low in Russia, and thus the uptake of PROCEED technologies is not likely in the near future.

China

As is the case in Russia, the development of underlying markets, notably for cloud computing and business service outsourcing, will predispose the adoption of PROCEED technologies in China. China's cloud infrastructure is robust and growing, though not nearly at a scale or sophistication present in the United States. The Chinese authorities have been actively involved in stimulating the development of all segments of the cloud computing markets.

Infrastructure-as-a-Service: The IaaS sector expanded sharply in 2011 and 2012, mainly because the local and national governments stimulated investment in public cloud infrastructure by establishing high-tech development zones and government grant programs (such as China's "863" program to procure advanced technologies from the West).[50] The market is dominated by several telecommunications giants: China Telecom, China Network Communications (CNC), China Mobile, China United Telecommunications, and 21ViaNET,[51] who signed contracts with many regional governments to build a

---

[49] Maria Popova and Lyubov Baydalina, "Рынок SaaS в России разгоняется и нагревается" ["Russia's SaaS Market Is Accelerating and Is Getting Hotter"], CNews Analytics, 2011.

[50] Hongjing Ma, 2011中国云计算市场研究报告-计世资讯 [*Research Report on China Cloud Computing Market*], July 22. 2011.

[51] The company's English website is at http://www.en.21vianet.com/ (21Vianet Group, Inc., 2010).

"public cloud" with grant support and also launched a product called CloudEx to provide server space and management for big online sites, such as gaming sites. In 2008, the central government designated five pilot "public cloud" computing development cities (Beijing, Shanghai, Hangzhou, Wuxi, and Shenzhen) mainly in the form of IaaS. Since then, the central government has allocated large sums to programs to support cloud infrastructure.[52] Current capitalization of the SaaS sector is estimated to be $85.17 million (511 million RMB) (Table 3.4).

Software-as-a-Service: The SaaS sector is dominated by the U.S. companies, such as HP, Intel, EMC, Sun, and IBM, with whom China's local officials signed contracts to establish regional data centers, develop testing platforms for software and government services, and facilitate knowledge transfer at regional R&D centers (such as the Peking University cloud computing center).[53] SaaS accounts for the single biggest slice of cloud computing market shares in China—as of 2010, its total revenue reached $583 million (3.5 billion RMB) in 2012 (Table 4.4).

Platform-as-a-Service: The PaaS sector in 2011 is the least developed sector and in 2012 accounted for only $30 million (184 million RMB). Its growth has been closely tied to the rapid expansion of e-commerce, with Taobao, Alibaba, Google, and Baidu being major providers of e-commerce services. [54] Baidu, for instance, invested $1.6 billion into a new cloud computing center[55] primarily to develop its own mobile applications and online document services. The use of public clouds by PaaS has been constrained by the lack of standards for

---

[52] A detailed description of these five programs can be found in Xi lin ge le Development Reform Committee, 关于五个试点城市发展云计算情况的调研报告 [*Report on the Pilot Cloud Computing Programs in Five Cities*], June 4, 2012.

[53] Various estimates have the total revenue of China's cloud computing in 2010 to be in the range between $2.6 billion and $8.6 billion. And in 2013, the cloud computing market will reach 16.7 billion yuan ($2.6 billion). CCID Consulting, "中国云计算产业发展白皮书" ["China Cloud Computing Industry Development White Paper"], April 2011.

[54] Chinese Government Purchase Center, "中国PaaS市场逐渐上升" ["China PaaS Market Is Gradually Increased"], December 12, 2012.

[55] Terril Jones, "China's Baidu to Invest $1.6 Billion to Set Up Cloud Computing Center," Reuters, September 3, 2012.

common cloud computing protocols among major e-commerce platform providers. [56]

Conclusion

This chapter has provided an overview of theoretical literature on the role of trust in business transactions, especially in the situations when economic actors cannot monitor each other's effort, and also substantiated it with empirical evidence on the demand for information on data protection and encryption among Internet users in Russia and China. The theoretical literature suggests that trust facilitates business transaction by reducing the cost of monitoring. Both the cost of monitoring how the trusted party protects sensitive information and the cost of using either FHE or SMP are high. Therefore, businesses are more likely to decide to adopt PROCEED technology when they do not completely trust each other and when the cost of monitoring how data are handled exceeds additional processing costs incurred via the use of FHE or SMP.

The insights from the game theoretic literature were supplemented by the empirical analysis of correlation between different types of trust and population demand for information about data encryption in Russia and China. In China, the demand for information about data encryption is higher in regions with lower levels of interpersonal trust, whereas in Russia the demand for information about data and information protection is higher in regions with lower levels of trust toward the government and law enforcement officials.

This suggests that the diffusion of PROCEED technologies in China will by stimulated by cultural factors, which remain persistent over time, and in Russia by popular attitudes toward authorities, which are less resilient. In both countries, the governments tightly regulate the encryption technology markets. Overall, we concluded that if the

---

[56] Wu Weih Ha, "[Research on Development Patterns of EC Based on Cloud Computing"] (Chinese translation), *Journal of Intelligence*, Vol. 30, No. 5, May 2011.

government approves the use of PROCEED technologies, their diffusion will be more rapid in China than in Russia.

CHAPTER FOUR

Where Will PROCEED Be Taken Up?

Having discussed how nuanced and contingent the trust model associated with PROCEED is (Chapter Two) and then the relative orientation toward encryption in Russia and China (Chapter Three), we now turn to make judgments on whether technologies that allow processing on encrypted data are more likely to benefit the United States (more generally, the West) than they are to benefit authoritarian states. The benefit may be measured by the extent of uptake multiplied by the degree of benefit for each application—but in practice can be proxied by uptake alone.

The usual caveats apply to such an exercise, but in this case more so. Most of the technology is, as of late 2013, still in development. The closest that a proto PROCEED technology has come to implementation (as far as publicly known) has been to administer Denmark's sugar beet auction using an information-theoretic secret-sharing–based protocol (BGW). By the time that PROCEED technologies achieve the kind of economics required to induce usage, the world of computation may be far different than it is today. Even the politics of encryption may change; indeed, it has changed considerably in 2013 alone as a result of press reports on the National Security Agency (NSA). The assumption that democratic states would tolerate an encryption-cum-anonymization service such as Tor even as authoritarian states would forbid it is not cast in steel; again, press reports indicate that the NSA has been quite active in finding out how to detect Tor users of interest.[1]

---

[1] Japan's police, for instance, are now calling for a ban on Tor (Ian Steadman, "Japanese Police Ask ISPs to Start Blocking Tor," *Ars Technica*, April 21, 2013).

In our assessment we distinguish between, first, political and, second, economic factors. According primacy to political factors may seem odd when the decision to adopt or not adopt any technology rests on whether a business case for adoption makes sense. But starting with the political distinction is consistent with trying to distinguish the rate of uptake in the United States and similar countries vis-à-vis uptake in advanced authoritarian countries—groups most keenly distinguished from the West by their political differences.

Political Factors

Three political factors may predispose the United States to employ PROCEED technologies more quickly and more completely than authoritarian states will:

1. the emphasis on the autonomy of individuals (and organizations) vis-à-vis the state, which prevents the latter from seizing any information it wants
2. the need to exchange communications with coalition partners
3. the need to create lawful surveillance tools that operate within the U.S. Constitution.

Autonomy: Underlying the Constitution, there are fundamental differences in the relationship between the citizen and the state in the United States (and Europe) vis-à-vis authoritarian countries. In the United States, the state is a social convention whose raison d'être is to serve citizens with more efficiency and fairness than alternative social constructs might. This is not to deny that even in democratic states, law enforcement and national security agencies might not walk to the not-always-unambiguously-defined edge of what is (in the United States) Constitutionally permitted. However, those wishing to keep their own secrets still have many avenues to pursue with warranted hopes that their efforts will succeed (or at least not visibly fail). It is possible that controversy over the NSA (and reports of its newly revealed access to the nation's trunk lines) may persuade more people to routinely prac-

tice end-to-end encryption. If so, this may prep the market for computing on such data as well.

In authoritarian states, the collective national will that the state
represents is the core social construct, and the people serve the goals of
the state (or the country it governs, or the collective will on whose behalf
it works). Granted, this is a caricature in the sense that many authoritarian states have adopted democratic forms (Russia, for instance, has
voting). Yet, when it comes down to a battle between the rights of the
citizen and the responsibilities of the state (as the state sees them), the
latter almost always wins. Authoritarian states count on their citizens
identifying themselves with the state ("if you've done nothing wrong,
why hide anything?") rather than with the individual citizen ("next
time, it could be me") if the two conflict. The right of the citizen to
keep a private life and therefore private information exists only insofar
as such privacy serves the needs of the state—which, in practice, means
only so long as it costs the state more to extract such information than
the state gains. Thus, the right to encrypt only means the right to keep
information from private entities, not the right to keep information
from the state.

Under such circumstances, the state has no need to see its citizens
suffer the processing penalties associated with computing on encrypted
data. If it does so, it does so as a courtesy that it can afford to extend,
but one that it could just as easily withdraw should its needs change.
Citizens have little right to resist and may be culpable if they resist by
denying that any such data exist. Such circumstances do not necessarily mean that two private entities cannot work together with encrypted
data. In practice, though, many such organizations are either state-
owned (as in China), state-influenced (as in Russia), or embedded in
well-understood hierarchical relationships in which patterns of defer-
ence are clear (so that one party can effectively demand to see the data
of another party if there is an interworking requirement).

Encryption, as such, is inseparably linked to the concepts of
ownership and autonomy. The existence of a market for processing
on encrypted data requires a sufficient population of data owners that
want to thread the path between too little trust (wherein no data are
exchanged, in part, because working relationships cannot be estab-

lished) and too much trust (wherein no data are encrypted). The autonomy and ownership necessary to make these nuanced choices are more likely to exist in Western environments than they are in authoritarian states.

Reactions to (reported) revelations about NSA activities may persuade more organizations to use encryption and keep their own keys. The reports have already persuaded Google to make encryption an easier default method.[2] Those who keep their information encrypted (as long as it is encrypted in certain ways) are thus one step closer to using PROCEED technologies, at least in the sense that they would now have to expose their data to the cloud provider (and thus create a theoretical risk of exposing their data to the U.S. government) if they would have the cloud provider carry out computations on this data *without* using PROCEED technologies.

Coalition partners: Working with coalition partners involves some complicated trade-offs. There are many reasons to want to know a great deal about them. Knowing what assets they could bring to the battlefield would allow U.S. forces to carry out combined planning with them in areas including logistics, medical care, combined ground operations, electronic warfare coverage, and air superiority (to name a few). Requests for allied data may also feed into near–real-time decisions to attempt a particular operation, reshape it, or call it off.

Such partners, however, may be reluctant to share their data very widely. They may not necessarily be allies (e.g., Syria during Operation Desert Storm). They may have information that they want to keep from the United States in case they do not remain U.S. allies. They may be instinctually reluctant to share information. They may fear that revealing their assets will lead to further requests or embarrass them for not having provided enough. They may reasonably figure that sharing data with the United States actually means sharing data with everyone with whom the United States shares—thereby multiplying the odds that the information will leak.

---

[2] David Linthicum, "Google's Cloud Encryption Is Good for PR—and Users, Too," *Info-World*, August 20, 2013.

PROCEED technologies, as mentioned in Chapter One, can enable the use of coalition partners' data in calculations carried out by or for the United States without having to reveal the data. The data of such partners would be relatively secure (relatively, because, as Chapter Two notes, it is possible to poke at the data several times and thereby get a sense of its bounds). The drawbacks to this arrangement are fairly obvious. Complex calculations will be considerably slower, but, more importantly, every use of the data that has not been converted into a form that PROCEED technologies can use would require generating a new algorithm—meaning that on-the-fly inquiries have to be ruled out. The saving grace, however, is that on-the-fly operations with the kind of coalition partners that would insist on encrypting their data are of limited importance; military operations are often intensively planned and rehearsed these days.

Over the last 20 years, the United States has worked with more coalition partners than either Russia or China has; there is little chance that the reverse will be true over the next 20 years, given current geopolitical realities and the importance of combined warfare in U.S. strategy. Furthermore, although allies are more likely to openly share data with the United States than coalition partners would, their willingness may be tempered in the future. The United States is a member of multiple alliances in ways that Russia and China are not. Rogue states such as Iran and North Korea have far fewer allies. Overall, therefore, such an application of PROCEED technologies is likely to help the United States earlier and more definitively than would be the case for other governments.

Lawful surveillance tools: PROCEED technologies may allow government agencies to process information for the purposes of surveillance without looking at the data. In this way the privacy of the American is preserved; correspondingly, the confidentiality of the instruments by which the U.S. government protects the nation can also be preserved. If the processing indicates that a record is of interest, the United States may be able to make a probable-cause argument for releasing the full record, without violating Constitutional provisions.

One example might be a set of emails that indicate possible participation in a crime. These emails are held in encrypted form by an Internet service provider. Law enforcement officials devise an algorithm that contains information that they want to keep private (it may also involve sensitive information that they are not allowed to reveal publicly without good cause). A circuit-based algorithm is devised that can process the encrypted email together with the encrypted sensitive search and return those emails whose contents can be reasonably disclosed after some minimization, probable cause, or sufficient specificity tests have been passed. Algorithms for private searching on encrypted data can be made significantly more quickly than many of the general-purpose computations considered in the PROCEED program. Currently, the Intelligence Advanced Research Projects Activity's (IARPA's) Security and Privacy Assurance Research (SPAR) Program is working to develop prototype software for applications of this sort.

As the example suggests, although the U.S. Constitution (notably the Fourth Amendment) is the cornerstone of the principle that mitigates against fishing expeditions, there are other laws—some on the books now, and some that may be anticipated as a reaction to the increasing pervasiveness of data collection—that constrain behavior. Such laws may require law enforcement (and intelligence) officials to pre-filter their searches in order to conform to popular sentiment that protects the innocent from detailed surveillance of their activities. Eric Schmidt and Jared Cohen's *The New Digital Age: Reshaping the Future of People, Nations and Business* (2013), for instance, posits that "We'll use computers to run predictive correlations from huge volumes of data to track and catch terrorists, but how they are interrogated and handled thereafter will remain the purview of humans and their laws." If such activity were to use sensitive criteria generated by the law enforcement community, then PROCEED technologies may be a way for the government to approach the challenge of preserving privacy while meeting law enforcement needs (bandwidth and processing speeds permitting). Indeed, if authorities associated with the transfer of such data know about PROCEED technologies, then they may then require these technologies be used, when otherwise they might have allowed unencrypted data to be used because the alternative would have been to prevent data exchange altogether. Thus, the cost of data processing would go up because the technology exists to meet what would otherwise be secondary criteria, albeit by creating new costs.

Authoritarian states in general, and Russia and China in particular, operate under no such constraints. Such countries have adopted many of the notional rules of procedure that the United States has, but neither country has an independent judiciary system, and thus no serious basis by which misbehavior of authorities can be called to account. In such countries, there is little question that if the state wanted to look at massed data it could do so. As a practical matter, however, if people know that they can be compelled to provide information at any time, they may forego collecting or generating it.

What PROCEED technologies permit the U.S. governments to do is to achieve *some* of the information-gathering benefits that authoritarian governments can achieve without the need to work on encrypted data. In other words, PROCEED technologies are a tool that authoritarian governments do not need because such governments are not troubled by questions of privacy or autonomy. For democratic governments, PROCEED technologies allow the production of useful information while respecting these values, or at least adhering to these values when it comes time to justify their use in court. Thus, in this respect, their benefits accrue only to democratic societies.

Nevertheless, the fact that PROCEED technologies can protect individual privacy and autonomy in ways that satisfy mathematicians does not necessarily imply that it can do so in ways that satisfy the courts. There are several ways in which an application to use private or proprietary data can be rejected. First, the courts may argue that the law simply did not make provisions for the data to be transferred even if it was encrypted (in other words, neither law nor precedent mentioned encryption). Second, some courts may simply refuse to accept the validity of mathematical proof vis-à-vis legal arguments (many have a hard enough time understanding basic tenets of probability theory). Third, courts may accept the possibility that encrypted data are not tantamount to search and seizure and may accept mathematical proofs, but they may not believe that sufficient proof has been made that the relevant protocols can be guaranteed to protect the information to a sufficiently high level.

Economic Factors

In contrast with political factors that strongly predispose the greater and more valuable use of PROCEED in the United States, the economic factors at most weakly predispose the use of PROCEED. We will discuss four relevant factors:

1. Business relationships in Western cultures tend to have higher levels of trust and therefore are more likely to fall within the nuanced zone where interworking is possible but outright data-sharing is inadvisable.

2. Software-based technologies, especially when they involve standards, tend to proliferate more quickly in the West than in the authoritarian areas of interest.

3. Forces of economic nationalism (driven, in part, by data privacy concerns) may persuade countries not to let personal data leave their borders, opening up a market for algorithms that can work with data that are exported from countries only in encrypted forms.

4. PROCEED technologies may benefit from network effects; as some parties begin to insist on using it, others may then have to use it to interwork with the former.

Business relationships: Data storage and processing entail transferring sensitive information from one actor (principal) to another (agent). Monitoring how the agent handles the data is costly, and data leaks are difficult to detect. So, PROCEED technologies may be sought when both sides need to reduce the level of trust required for the two parties to engage in the transaction. Interest in encryption is correlated with trust, but in two opposite ways: The more trust the greater the tendency to work with others, but the less trust the greater the desire to encrypt the information that others might handle. After having examined the correlation between trust and the demand for information about data encryption, data protection, and IT security in Russia and China, it became apparent that the levels of demand for PROCEED in Russia and China would diverge. The demand for PROCEED technologies in Russia will be influenced by political conditions that affect overall trust toward the government and law enforcement officials, whereas in China, cultural norms will shape the diffusion of PROCEED technologies. Markets for encryption are more mature in China than in Russia. Encryption in general, and FHE in particular, is under discussion by only a handful of Internet users in Russia. In China, the demand for information about encryption is as high as that for data protection. PROCEED technologies are likely to see mass adoption in China before they see mass adoption in Russia, but neither would necessarily precede U.S. adoption.

Standards: There are very few areas of software that can thrive without some sort of standardization, be it *de jure* (e.g., the Institute of Electrical and Electronics Engineers) or *de facto* (e.g., Microsoft's document formats). This is particularly important in cryptography, which often relies on a series of handshakes to ensure, for instance, that keys are exchanged correctly and appropriately. At this juncture, most of the standards that govern cyberspace are of U.S. origin, partially for historic reasons (e.g., the Internet was invented here) and partially because U.S. firms dominate the world's packaged software (and web services) industry. In cryptography, by way of example, the two dominant standard setters are the National Institute of Standards and Technology (NIST), which is a U.S. government agency (e.g., it specified the Advanced Encryption Standard [AES]), and RSA (a U.S.-headquartered firm). This development does not necessarily arise because the United States dominates the production of world-class software engineers (Russia's and India's are very good as well), but because standards require convergence, and the United States still hosts the world's most natural convergence point in information technology.[3]

That noted, the adoption of PROCEED technologies is likely to take place in pairs engaged in two-party computations or, at most, among small groups (e.g., as contributors to a larger dataset or as suspicious customers of a particular cloud vendor). New technologies have to compete against established technologies and thus need standards

---

[3] How well this leadership survives reports that the NSA has had some less-than-benign influence on cryptography standards remains to be determined.

to overcome the latter's embedded advantages. But those who adopt PROCEED technologies are likely to want them badly enough to put up with the performance penalty that their use entails. In many ways, standards lag behind the markets they help rather than lead them. Against this, the lack of standardization would not be that much of a deal-breaker, at least while PROCEED's adoption was on the flat slope below the S-curve. Furthermore, even if standardization were critical, the dominance of U.S. and Western firms in the standards-setting process only means that the U.S. use of PROCEED technologies would be just a few years ahead of similar usage curves in Russia and China.

For this reason, the U.S. standardization advantage is likely to be no more than a weak positive differentiator between adoption in the United States and adoption in authoritarian states.

Economic nationalism: Starting in the 1980s, European countries mandated that European data be subject to strict provisions regarding their collection, transfer, and disposal. Along with such laws, Europe forbad the export of data to countries where these laws were not in force, permitting "safe harbor" exemptions for U.S. companies who pledged to follow such standards. Europeans, in general, have maintained a more suspicious attitude toward data collection organizations, with Google being a particular bête noire in Brussels.

If such trends strengthen and deepen (not a sure thing), one can easily imagine that countries would forbid certain types of data to cross their borders, thereby inhibiting the development of services that require the amalgamation of data or data services across borders in order to work efficiently, if at all.[4] In such a world, PROCEED technologies may play an especially important role if sensitive countries can be convinced by cryptographers that data leaving their countries (technically, leaving the enclave in which a country's data rules apply and traveling to a zone in which they do not) in encrypted form remain protected from disclosure. Such service companies may put up with high processing penalties to be able to access such data at all (the obvi-

---

[4] See, for instance, Danny Hakim, "Europe Aims to Regulate the Cloud," *New York Times*, October 6, 2013.

ous drawback is that data analysis is already so processor-intensive that it cannot stand much in the way of additional processing penalties).

Were such conditions to prevail, would the United States (with its, at best, heterogeneous and idiosyncratic laws on the subject), or perhaps the West in general, be able to exploit the value of PROCEED technologies before and beyond their exploitation in autocratic countries? It would seem so. We presume that Europe's sensitivities reflect popular pressure as translated by the legislative process, and the United States trades more with Europe than authoritarian states do. But two other considerations merit note:

1. While the volume of information trade with Europe is higher for the United States than it is for authoritarian countries, Europe may have fewer qualms about sharing its data with the United States in this hypothetical future (thereby obviating the need for PROCEED technologies) than it has about sharing data with authoritarian countries (thereby creating the need for PROCEED technologies).

2. Economic nationalism may come more easily to authoritarian governments who can use the fear of America's big-data companies (e.g., Google) as an excuse to foster home-grown alternatives. Overall, it would appear that the cross-border data restrictions and the use of PROCEED technologies to work through these restrictions would be more likely in the West than in authoritarian states, but it is a close call.

Diffusion: If two organizations adopt a set of conventions for dealing with one another, the chances rise that they will request that similar conventions be adopted to deal with third parties. PROCEED technologies, as interaction technologies, are likely to have network effects (once they prove themselves useful). The relationship between diffusion and usage patterns and geographic region is complex. Internet use rose more rapidly in the United States (in terms of net additions per year) than it did overseas in the 1980s and 1990s for precisely such reasons—but then Internet use rose more quickly overseas as the latter played catch-up. Since PROCEED technologies are a much better fit for organizations than for individuals, their uptake patterns are likely to follow trade (more precisely, data exchange) paths modified by the likelihood that the appropriate partners for such interactions would be those that are partially trusted (fully trusted partners can enjoy unencumbered data exchange, while untrusted partners get little or no exchange). This would lead to wider, if not faster, diffusion patterns than those that characterized the Internet. Over time, diffusion patterns are likely to reduce the difference between democratic states and those authoritarian states whose organizations (e.g., corporations) are networked to Western organizations—but widen the difference between democratic states and authoritarian states that sit apart from Western organizations.

Conclusion

We cannot determine whether PROCEED technologies will be adopted in the face of the processing penalties that will be associated with using them, even if DARPA's program meets its technical goals. Our assessment indicates that although the prospect of being able to combine data from multiple parties or use third-party services while keeping data protected is an attractive one, there are many alternatives to using PROCEED that allow potential customers to make a range of trade-offs between economics and security. Nevertheless, there are many use cases for which PROCEED may be favored.

We judge that if PROCEED is adopted, it is more likely to be adopted more rapidly in the United States (and similar developed countries) than it is in Russia and China, in large part because PROCEED is compatible with the U.S. political culture, and in smaller part because it better accords to the U.S. business environment.

Bibliography

21Vianet Group, Inc., home page, 2010. As of August 7, 2013:
http://www.en.21vianet.com/

2012 China Cloud Computing Summit, "The Advantages and Barriers of Cloud Computing Industry in China" ["云计算产业发展的优势与障碍"], eNet, 2012. As of August 7, 2013:
www.enet.com.cn/article/2012/0907/A20120907159634.shtml

Acemoglu, Daron, Azarakhsh Malekian, and Asu Ozdaglar, "Network Security and Contagion," NBER Working Paper No. 19174, June 18, 2013.

Al-Najjar, N. I., and R. Casadesus-Masanell, "Trust and Discretion in Agency Contracts," Harvard Business School Working Paper, April 2002. As of October 28, 2012:
http://www.people.hbs.edu/rmasanell/workpap/trust_and_discretion9.pdf

Anderson, Ross, "Why Information Security Is Hard: An Economic Perspective," Proceedings of the 17th Annual Computer Security Applications Conference, December 10–14, 2001. As of October 7, 2013:
www.acsac.org/2001/papers/110.pdf

Anderson, Ross, and Tyler Moore, "The Economics of Information Security," Science, Vol. 314, October 27, 2006.

Beshkov, Andrey, "Андрей Бешков: Безопасность в «облаке»" ["Andrey Beshkov: Safety in the 'Cloud'"], Cloudzone.ru, blog post, December 22, 2011. As of August 7, 2013:
cloudzone.ru/articles/expert_opinion/43.html

BSA, "Global Cloud Computing Scorecard: Russia," 2013. As of August 7, 2013:
http://cloudscorecard.bsa.org/2013/countries.html

Cambridge Advocate Legal News Services, "The Law on Liability for Violation of the Law on the Protection of Personal Data Came Into Effect," Newswire, July 24, 2011. As of March 20, 2013:
http://www.cleri.com.ru/news/
vstupil-v-silu-zakon-ob-usilenii-otvetstvennosti-za-narushen.html

Casadesus-Masanell, R., and D. F. Spulber, "Trust and Incentives in Agency," *South California Interdisciplinary Law Journal,* Vol. 15, No. 1, Fall 2005, pp. 45–104.

Cavusoglu, Huseyin, Srinivasan Rughunathan, and Wei T. Yue, "Decision-Theoretic and Game-Theoretic Approaches to IT Security Investment," *Journal of Management Information Systems*, Vol. 25, No. 2, Fall 2008, pp. 281–304.

CCID Consulting, "中国云计算产业发展白皮书" ["China Cloud Computing Industry Development White Paper"], April 2011. As of April 5, 2013: http://data.ccidconsulting.com/ei/lib/down/20110509154002.pdf

CCW Research [计世资讯], *2010–2011 China Cloud Computing Market Research Report* [中国云计算市场研究报告], 2010.

Central People's Government of the People's Republic of China, "中华人民共和国刑法修正案" ["The 7th Amendment to the Criminal Law of the People's Republic of China"], February 28, 2009. As of April 20, 2013: http://www.gov.cn/flfg/2009-02/28/content_1246438.htm

Chao, Loretta, "Beijing to Impose Encryption Disclosure Rules," *Wall Street Journal*, April 29, 2010. As of April 20, 2013: online.wsj.com/article/SB10001424052748704423504575211842948430882.html

Chin, Andrew, and Anne Klinefelter, "Differential Privacy as a Response to the Re-Identification Threat: The Facebook Advertiser Case Study," *North Carolina Law Review*, Vol. 90, No. 5, 2012.

China Academy of Telecommunication Research of MIIT, *China Cloud Computing White Book* [中国云计算白皮书], April 2012.

China E-Commerce Study Center [中国电子商务研究中心讯], "电商和云计算应用完美相结合" ["Electricity Supplier and the Perfect Combination of Cloud Computing Applications"], 2011. As of August 7, 2013: http://www.100ec.cn/detail--6002822.html

China E-Commerce Study Center [中国电子商务研究中心讯], "云计算给企业发展电子商务带来的机遇" ["Cloud Computing for E-Commerce Business Development"], 2012. As of August 7, 2013: http://b2b.toocle.com/detail--6018533.html

China Internet Network Information Center (CINIC), 中国互联网发展报告 (2013) [*The 32nd China Internet Development Statistics Report, 2013*], July 2013. As of April 21, 2014: http://www.isc.org.cn/download/baogao2013.pdf

Chinese Government Purchase Center, "中国PaaS市场逐渐上升" ["China PaaS Market Is Gradually Increased"], December 12, 2012. As of December 12, 2012: http://www.ccgp.gov.cn/gysh/itch/itzx/201212/t20121212_2511300.shtml

Cloutier, Christopher, and Jane Y. Cohen, "Casting a Wide Net: China's Encryption Regulation," *WorldECR*, November 2011. As of August 7, 2013: http://www.colorado.edu/vcr/sites/default/files/attached-files/ China%20Encryption%20Regulation.pdf

CNews Analytics, "Крупнейшие ИТ-компании России в сфере защиты информации" ["Largest IT Companies in Russia in the Area of Protection of Personal Data"], 2011. As of August 7, 2013: http://www.cnews.ru/reviews/free/security2011/ratings/rating1.shtml

CyberSecurity.ru, "Объем Рынка Шифрования Данных Удвоится В Предстоящие 5 Лет" ["The Russian Encryption Market Will Double in 5 Years"], April 12, 2013. As of October 14, 2013: http://www.cybersecurity.ru/crypto/173218.html

Damgård, Ivan, and Tomas Toft, "Trading Sugar Beet Quotas—Secure Multiparty Computation in Practice," *Ercim News 73: Maths in Everyday Life*, April 2008. As of June 13, 2014: http://ercim-news.ercim.eu/en73/special/ trading-sugar-beet-quotas-secure-multiparty-computation-in-practice

Dyachenko, Oksana, "Банки присматриваются к «облакам»" ["Banks Are Looking at the 'Cloud'"], *National Bank Journal*, July 24, 2012. As of August 7, 2013: www.klerk.ru/bank/articles/276626/

Ensminger, Jean, "Reputations, Trust, and the Principal Agent Problem," in Karen S. Cook, ed., *Trust in Society*, New York: Russell Sage Foundation, 2001, p. 199.

Esai Technologies, "2009年中国加密软件行业大势" ["The Trends of Chinese Encryption Software Industry as of 2009"], blog post, 51CTO, January 31, 2010. As of April 30, 2013: http://netsecurity.51cto.com/art/201001/181690.htm

Feigenbaum, Joan, Benny Pinkas, Raphael Ryger, and Felipe Saint-Jean, "Some Requirements for Adoption of Privacy-Preserving Data Mining," PORTIA Project White Paper, April 2005. As of June 13, 2014: http://www.cs.yale.edu/homes/jf/Requirements.pdf

FOM—*see* Foundation for Monitoring of Public Opinion.

Foundation for Monitoring of Public Opinion, *Monitoring of Socio-Economic Changes Survey*, 2008. As of June 13, 2014: http://sophist.hse.ru/db/oprview.shtml?ID_S=2050&T=m

Foundation for Monitoring of Public Opinion, "Защита персональных данных" ["Protection of Personal Data"], May 13, 2013. As of June 1, 2013: http://runet.fom.ru/SMI-i-internet/10922

Fukuyama, Francis, "Trust: The Social Virtues and the Creation of Prosperity," New York: Free Press, 1995.

Galvan, David A., Brett Hemenway, William Welser IV, and Dave Baiocchi, *Satellite Anomalies: Benefits of a Centralized Anomaly Database and Methods for Securely Sharing Information Among Satellite Operators*, Santa Monica, Calif.: RAND Corporation, RR-560-DARPA, 2014. As of June 13, 2014: http://www.rand.org/pubs/research_reports/RR560.html

Goldreich, O., S. Micali, and A. Wigderson, "How to Play Any Mental Game," *Symposium on the Theory of Computing (STOC) '87*, 1987, pp. 218–229. As of August 6, 2013: http://doi.acm.org/10.1145/28395.28420

Gordon, Lawrence A., and Martin P. Loeb, "The Economics of Information Security Investment," *ACM Transactions on Information and System Security*, Vol. 5, No. 4, November 2002, pp. 438–457. As of October 5, 2013: http://dl.acm.org/citation.cfm?id=581274

Goskomstat, *Regiony Rossii*, 2008. As of October 12, 2013: http://www.gks.ru/wps/wcm/connect/rosstat_main/rosstat/ru/statistics/publications/catalog/doc_1138623506156

Goyal, Vipul, Yuval Ishai, Amit Sahai, Ramarathnam Venkatesan, and Akshay Wadia, "Founding Cryptography on Tamper-Proof Hardware Tokens," *Theory of Cryptography: Lecture Notes in Computer Science*, Vol. 5978, 2010, pp. 308–326. As of August 6, 2013: http://link.springer.com/chapter/10.1007%2F978-3-642-11799-2_19

Grashenko, Kosntantin, "Бизнес обживает облака" ["Business Cloud Settles"], CRN, No. 3 (71), July 2, 2012. As of July 2, 2012: www.crn.ru/numbers/spec-numbers/detail.php?ID=66722

Grossklags, Jens, Nicolas Christin, and John Chuang, "Secure or Insure? A Game-Theoretic Analysis of Information Security Games," WWW 2008, April 21–22, 2008. As of October 4, 2013: www.andrew.cmu.edu/user/nicolasc/publications/GCC-WWW08.pdf

Guiso, Luigo, Paola Sapienza, and Luigi Zingales, "The Role of Social Capital in Financial Development," National Bureau of Economic Research, Working Paper 7563, February 2000.

Ha, Wu Weih, "[Research on Development Patterns of EC Based on Cloud Computing"] (Chinese translation), *Journal of Intelligence*, Vol. 30, No. 5, May 2011.

Habrahabr.ru, "Гомоморфное шифрование своими руками" ["Do It Yourself: Homomorphic Encryption"], blog post, August 23, 2012. As of August 7, 2013: http://habrahabr.ru/post/150067/#habracut

Hakim, Danny, "Europe Aims to Regulate the Cloud," *New York Times*, October 6, 2013. As of June 13, 2014:
http://www.nytimes.com/2013/10/07/business/international/europe-aims-to-regulate-the-cloud.html

Harney, Alexandra, "China's Copycat Culture," *New York Times,* 2011. As of August 7, 2013:
http://latitude.blogs.nytimes.com/2011/10/31/chinas-copycat-culture/

Hausken, Kjell, "Returns to Information Security Investment: The Effect of Alternative Information Security Breach Functions on Optimal Investment and Sensitivity to Vulnerability," *Information System Frontiers*, Vol. 8, No. 5, December 2006. As of October 5, 2013:
http://dl.acm.org/citation.cfm?id=1196618

Hemenway, Brett, William Welser IV, and Dave Baiocchi, *Achieving Higher-Fidelity Conjunction Analyses Using Cryptography to Improve Information Sharing*, Santa Monica, Calif.: RAND Corporation, RR-344-AF, 2014. As of June 13, 2014:
http://www.rand.org/pubs/research_reports/RR344.html

Hitmeter.ru, "Reyting Uspol'zuyemikh Poiskovikh System v Dekabre 2012" ["Ranking of the Most Popular Search Engines"], undated. As of October 8, 2013:
http://hitmeter.ru/stat/2012/12/2

Howorth, Carole, and Andrea Moro, "Trustworthiness and Interest Rates: An Empirical Study of Italian SMEs," *Small Business Economics,* Vol. 39, 2012, pp. 161–177.

"Доктрина информационной безопасности Российской Федерации" ["Information Security Doctrine of the Russian Federation"], *Rossiyskaya Gazeta*, undated. As of March 23, 2013:
http://www.rg.ru/oficial/doc/min_and_vedom/mim_bezop/doctr.shtm

Information Security Protection Administration, home page, June 22, 2007. As of August 7, 2013:
http://www.mps.gov.cn/n16/n1282/n3493/n3793/n494630/494907.html

International Data Corporation (IDC), "Quantitative Evidence of the Demand for Cloud Computing in Europe and the Likely Barriers to Adoption," 2011, p. 34. As of October 1, 2012:
ec.europa.eu/information_society/activities/cloudcomputing/docs/quantitative_estimates.pdf

J'son & Partners Consulting, "Российский рынок IaaS" ["Market Watch: Russian IaaS Market"], September 2013. As of October 12, 2013:
http://www.json.ru/poleznye_materialy/free_market_watches/analytics/rossijskij_rynok_iaas_2013/

Jackson, Jonathan, Nick Allum, and George Gaskell, "Perceptions of Risk in Cyberspace," in Robin Mansell and Brian S. Collins, eds., *Trust and Crime in Information Societies*, Cheltenham, UK: Edward Elgar, 2005, pp. 245–281.

Jones, Terril, "China's Baidu to Invest $1.6 Billion to Set Up Cloud Computing Center," Reuters, September 3, 2012. As of June 23, 2014:
www.reuters.com/article/2012/09/03/us-baidu-idUSBRE88203320120903

Kahneman, Daniel, *Thinking Fast and Slow*, Farrar, Straus and Giroux, 2012.

Kim, Anya, and Ira S. Moskowitz, "Incentivized Cloud Computing: A Principal Agent Solution to the Cloud Computing Dilemma," Naval Research Laboratory Report #NRL/MR/5540-10-9292, September 15, 2010. As of October 3, 2013:
http://oai.dtic.mil/oai/
oai?verb=getRecord&metadataPrefix=html&identifier=ADA530441

Knapper, Rico, Benjamin Blau, Tobias Conte, Anca Sailer, Andrzej Kochut, and Ajay Mohindra, "Efficient Contracting in Cloud Service Markets with Asymmetric Information: A Screening Approach," 2011 IEEE Conference on Commerce and Enterprise Computing, Luxembourg, Luxembourg, September 5–7, 2011, pp. 236–243. As of April 21, 2014:
http://www.computer.org/csdl/proceedings/cec/2011/4535/00/4535a236-abs.html

Ledeneva, Alena, *Russia's Economy of Favours: Blat, Networking and Informal Exchange*, Cambridge, UK: Cambridge University Press, 1998.

Libicki, Martin C., Brian A. Jackson, David R. Frelinger, Beth E. Lachman, Cesse Cameron Ip, and Nidhi Kalra, *What Should Be Classified? A Framework with Application to the Global Force Management Data Initiative*, Santa Monica, Calif.: RAND Corporation, MG-989-JS, 2010. As of April 22, 2014:
http://www.rand.org/pubs/monographs/MG989.html

Linthicum, David, "Google's Cloud Encryption Is Good for PR—and Users, Too," *InfoWorld*, August 20, 2013. As of June 23, 2014:
http://www.infoworld.com/d/cloud-computing/
googles-cloud-encryption-good-pr-and-users-too-225179

Ma, Hongjing, 2011中国云计算市场研究报告-计世资讯 [*Research Report on China Cloud Computing Market*], July 22, 2011. As of April 20, 2013:
http://share.tele.com.cn/share/download/id/576

Makarova, Anna, "Poiskoviye Systemy Runeta" ["RuNet Search Engines"], *Internet v Rossii* [*Internet in Russia*], Russian Association for Electronic Communications, June 2012. As of October 8, 2013:
http://www.raec.ru/2012/

Miller, Gary J., and Andrew B. Whitford, "Trust and Incentives in Principal-Agent Negotiations: The 'Insurance/Incentive Trade-Off,'" *Journal of Theoretical Politics*, Vol. 14, No. 2, 2002, pp. 231–267.

The Ministry of Public Safety of People's Republic of China, "信息安全等级保护管理办法 (公通字[2007]43号)" ["Information Security Protection Management Regulations, [2007] No. 43"], June 22, 2007. As of April 29, 2013: http://www.mps.gov.cn/n16/n1282/n3493/n3793/n494630/494907.html

Moore, Geoffrey A., *Crossing the Chasm: Marketing and Selling Disruptive Products to Mainstream Customers,* New York: Harper Collins Books, 1991.

"Ob'yem Rynka Shifrovaniya Dannykh Udvoitsya za 5 Let" ["The Market for Data Encryption will Double in 5 Years"], CyberSecurity.ru, 2013. As of June 4, 2013:
http://www.cybersecurity.ru/crypto/173218.html

People's Liberty Army Daily, "广州军区研制涉密数据安全保护系统" ["Guangzhou Military District Conducts Research on Classified Data Protection System"], October 25, 2006. As of October 25, 2013:
http://mil.qianlong.com/4919/2006/10/25/2420@3476284.htm

Popova, Maria, and Lyubov Baydalina, "Рынок SaaS в России разгоняется и нагревается" ["Russia's SaaS Market Is Accelerating and Is Getting Hotter"], CNews Analytics, 2011. As of October 17, 2013:
http://www.cnews.ru/reviews/free/saas/articles/articles1.shtml

Research and Markets, "Cost Reduction with Rising Internet Use Drives the Chinese Cloud Computing Market, Finds Netscribes," Business Wire (English), March 2005. Available from Regional Business News, Ipswich, Mass., as of September 6, 2012.

Roberts, Hal, Ethan Zuckerman, Jillian York, Robert Faris, and John Palfrey, *2010 Circumvention Tool Usage Report*, Berkman Center, October 2010.

Robertson, Jordan, "Why Google Isn't Winning in Russia," *Global Tech*, April 26, 2013. As of October 1, 2013:
http://www.bloomberg.com/news/2013-04-26/
why-google-isn-t-winning-in-russia.html

"Russian Laws and Regulations: Implications for Kaspersky Labs," *Wired*, February 2013. As of April 21, 2014:
http://www.wired.com/images_blogs/dangerroom/2012/07/
Russian-Laws-and-Regulations-and-Implications-for-Kaspersky-Labs.pdf

Schmidt, Eric, and Jared Cohen, *The New Digital Age: Reshaping the Future of People, Nations and Business*, Knopf, April 2013.

Schneier, Bruce, "Terms of Service as a Security Threat," December 31, 2012. As of October 16, 2013:
https://www.schneier.com/blog/archives/2012/12/

Sina Tech, "关于出台《个人信息数据保护法》的提案" ["A Proposal: The Personal Information Protection and Data Protection Bill, Introduced by Democratic National Construction Association Central Committee Vice Chairman Chen Li"], March 8, 2006. As of October 25, 2013:
http://tech.sina.com.cn/i/2006-03-08/1751861508.shtml

Sincha, Oleg, "За 4 года рынок облачных услуг в РФ вырастет почти на 330%" ["Russia's Cloud Market Will Grow in 4 Times Over the Next 4 Years"], blog post summarizing Orange Business Survey Report, February 20, 2013. As of October 17, 2013:
http://digit.ru/business/20130220/399180233.html

Southern News Industry Network, "粤拟投资六亿保护社保数据" ["Guangdong Province Plans to Invest ¥600 Million to Protect Social Security Data"], December 26, 2006. As of December 26, 2012:
http://news.163.com/06/1227/09/33BEHD8L000120GU.html

Steadman, Ian, "Japanese Police Ask ISPs to Start Blocking Tor," *Ars Technica*, April 21, 2013. As of August 7, 2013:
arstechnica.com/tech-policy/2013/04/
japanese-police-ask-isps-to-start-blocking-tor/

Sweeney, L., "Simple Demographics Often Identify People Uniquely," Carnegie Mellon University, Data Privacy Working Paper 3, Pittsburgh, 2000. As of August 6, 2013:
http://dataprivacylab.org/projects/identifiability/paper1.pdf

TOPS Business Integrator, "Аналитика рынка ИБ в России 2010–2011 гг" ["Analysis of IT Security Market in Russia 2010–2011"], undated. As of April 1, 2013:
http://www.topsbi.ru/defult.asp?artID=1927&mode=print

"Tsifra Nedeli: 38% Rossiyskikh Kompaniy ne Zabotatsya o Shifrovanii Korporotovnykh Dannykh" ["News of the Week: 38 Percent of Russian Companies Do Not Encrypt Their Data"], April 3, 2013. As of June 1, 2013:
http://www.kaspersky.ru/news?id=207733979

Vlasov, Alexandr, "Security Market in Russia Keeps Growing in Spite of the Crisis," Groteck Business Media, Global Security Mag, August 2010. As of June 23, 2014:
https://www.globalsecuritymag.fr/
Security-market-in-Russia-keeps,20100818,19014.html

"Vstupil Zakon ob Usiliniye Otvetstvennosty za Narusheniye Zakonodatelstava o Zashite Personalnykh Dannykh," As of August 7, 2013:
http://www.cleri.com.ru/news/
vstupil-v-silu-zakon-ob-usilenii-otvetstvennosti-za-narushen.html

Wilson, Kristina, Yaneli Ramos, and Daniel Harvey, "Google in China: The Great Firewall," The Kenan Institute for Ethics, Duke University, undated. As of October 11, 2013:
https://web.duke.edu/kenanethics/CaseStudies/GoogleInChina.pdf

World Bank, "Economic Development Indicators," 2013. As of October 2, 2013:
http://data.worldbank.org/indicator/NY.GDP.PCAP.CD

Xi lin ge le Development Reform Committee, 关于五个试点城市发展云计算情况的调研报告 [*Report on the Pilot Cloud Computing Programs in Five Cities*], June 4, 2012. As of May 1, 2013:
http://www.xlgldrc.gov.cn/gzdt/vzhgggzdt/201206/t20120604_796563.html

Xilin Gol League Development and Reform Commission, "关于五个试点城市发展云计算情况的调研报告" ["Investigation Report on the Five Pilot Cities in the Development of Cloud Computing Situations"], June 2012. As of August 7, 2013:
http://www.xlgldrc.gov.cn/gzdt/vzhgggzdt/201206/t20120604_796563.html

Xinhuanet, "刑法修正案草案 单位泄露公民个人信息将追究刑责" ["The Draft Amendment to the Criminal Law Unit Divulge Personal Information of Citizens Will Be Held Criminally Liable"], February 25, 2009. As of June 13, 2014:
http://news.xinhuanet.com/newscenter/2009-02/25/content_10895635.htm

XJTU, Chinese Blue Book for Cloud Computing Safety Policy and Laws (中国云计算安全政策与法律蓝皮书), Xi'an Jiaotong University, October 14, 2011.

Yandex.ru, keyword search stats (in Russian), undated. As of April 21, 2014:
http://wordstat.yandex.ru

Yao, Andrew, "Protocols for Secure Computations," SFCS '82, Proceedings of the 23rd Annual Symposium on Foundations of Computer Science, Chicago, Ill., November 3–5, 1982, pp. 160–164.

Yao, Andrew, "How to Generate and Exchange Secrets," SFCS '86, Proceedings of the 27th Annual Symposium on Foundations of Computer Science, Toronto, Ontario, Canada, October 27–29, 1986, pp. 162–167.